Earthquake Prediction and Public Policy

Prepared by the
PANEL ON THE PUBLIC POLICY IMPLICATIONS
OF EARTHQUAKE PREDICTION
of the
ADVISORY COMMITTEE ON EMERGENCY PLANNING
Commission on Sociotechnical Systems
National Research Council

NATIONAL ACADEMY OF SCIENCES
WASHINGTON, D.C. 1975

NOTICE: The project that is the subject of this report was approved by the Governing Board of the National Research Council, acting in behalf of the National Academy of Sciences. Such approval reflects the Board's judgment that the project is of national importance and appropriate with respect to both the purposes and resources of the National Research Council.

The members of the committee selected to undertake this project and prepare this report were chosen for recognized scholarly competence and with due consideration for the balance of disciplines appropriate to the project. Responsibility for the detailed aspects of this report rests with that committee.

Each report issuing from a study committee of the National Research Council is reviewed by an independent group of qualified individuals according to procedures established and monitored by the Report Review Committee of the National Academy of Sciences. Distribution of the report is approved by the President of the Academy upon satisfactory completion of the review process.

This study was sponsored by the Advisory Committee on Emergency Planning, Commission on Sociotechnical Systems, and is submitted to the Federal Disaster Assistance Administration of the Department of Housing and Urban Development under provisions of Contract H-3664 between the National Academy of Sciences and the Federal Disaster Assistance Administration, Department of Housing and Urban Development.

The National Research Council was established in 1916 by the National Academy of Sciences to associate the broad community of science and technology with the Academy's purposes of furthering knowledge and of advising the federal government. The Council operates in accordance with general policies determined by the Academy by authority of its Congressional charter of 1863, which establishes the Academy as a private, non-profit, self-governing membership corporation. Administered jointly by the National Academy of Sciences, the National Academy of Engineering, and the Institute of Medicine (all three of which operate under the charter of the National Academy of Sciences), the Council is their principal agency for the conduct of their services to the government, the public, and the scientific and engineering communities.

Library of Congress Cataloging in Publication Data
National Research Council. Panel on the Public Policy Implications of Earthquake Prediction.
 Earthquake prediction and public policy.

 Includes bibliographical references.
 1. Earthquake prediction. 2. Earthquakes—United States. 3. United States—Civil defense. I. Title.
 QE535.2.U6N37 1975   363.'34   75-31953
 ISBN 0-309-02404-8

Available from
Printing and Publishing Office, National Academy of Sciences
2101 Constitution Avenue, N.W., Washington, D.C. 20418

Printed in the United States of America

Preface

The Panel on the Public Policy Implications of Earthquake Prediction, working under the Advisory Committee on Emergency Planning, was established in April 1974. The Panel was mandated to:

provide advice to the Federal Disaster Assistance Administration, Department of Housing and Urban Development, that will serve as a basis for the formulation of public policy relating to an expected earthquake prediction capability. The types of governmental response with which the Panel will be concerned include warning of public officials and of the general public; governmental actions to mitigate the loss of life and property; and the need for further studies and research.

The Panel's responsibilities complement those of the Panel on Earthquake Prediction, under the Committee on Seismology of the National Research Council, which is conducting a state-of-the-art assessment of the physical science aspects of earthquake prediction. The present report draws upon preliminary analyses conducted by that group.

The Panel report is intended for use by decision makers in federal, state, and local governments and in private agencies; by leaders in the business community and other parts of the private sector; by scientists and engineers concerned with disaster prevention, mitigation, and preparedness; and by interested citizens.

Earthquake prediction is a new and unstudied field, and analogies to better-understood disaster-warning situations are often imperfect. Consequently, many of our conclusions and recommendations must be advanced quite tentatively. Panel members view their chief contributions as identifying and clarifying important social, economic, legal, and political issues that may arise as we attempt to make constructive use of the new prediction capability. Whenever warranted by our current understanding, we recommend specific courses of action to be followed by public and private officials and by individuals. But mastery of a few directives to action can be only a very poor substitute for a thorough comprehension of the complexities and uncertainties surrounding the social and economic consequences of earthquake prediction.

Earthquake prediction technology and theory are developing rapidly as this report is being released. Experience with actual predictions of potentially destructive earthquakes will immeasurably improve our comprehension of the social and economic dynamics of prediction. Hence there will be important differences between responses to the first and later predictions. But in both cases, preparation *now* for future predictive capability should greatly improve the chances for responding constructively to save lives and property and to maintain public order.

Although the first successful prediction of a minor quake occurred in the state of New York, the most rapid progress toward establishing an operational prediction capability is occurring in California. We look toward the California experience as a prototype, but our concern is that the rest of the United States should profit from that experience. The threat of earthquakes exists in most of the states, and earthquake prediction may eventually be a valuable tool in reducing the earthquake toll in many parts of the country.

Our report deals extensively with the role of government agencies in responding to earthquake predictions. But our analyses indicate that constructive use of the period of advance warning will depend largely on wholehearted participation and leadership from the private sector. Many of the most troublesome prospects in the economic sphere can be dealt with effectively only through cooperative planning by leaders of business, finance, and labor working together with government officials.

The conclusions and recommendations have been placed first in the report, for emphasis. Chapter 2 begins our analysis with an examination of the socially significant characteristics of earthquake prediction. Chapter 3 identifies the principal hazards from earthquakes and outlines the strategy for dealing with them on the basis of advance warning. Chapter 4 is an effort to anticipate how people will respond to an earthquake warning and to suggest guidelines for the release of predictions and warnings. Chapter 5 explores some of the economic aspects of the response to prediction, and Chapter 6 examines important legal issues and problems. Chapter 7 calls attention to the probability that the costs and inconveniences of earthquakes and prediction will fall disproportionately on some population segments. Chapter 8 examines some of the implications of the political process for development of a constructive response to prediction, and Chapter 9 summarizes the major ways in which earthquake prediction can be used to reduce the loss of life, the destruction of property, and the social disruption of the community.

The Panel gratefully acknowledges the valuable information and consultation contributed by the liaison representatives, by three political scientists—Stanley Scott, Robert Warren, and Alan J. Wyner—and by Charles E. Fritz, Executive Secretary of the Advisory Committee on Emergency Planning. Gratitude is also expressed for the editorial services performed by Sarah Osgood Brooks.

ADVISORY COMMITTEE ON EMERGENCY PLANNING

JAMES F. THORNTON, *Chairman,* Chairman of the Board, The Lummus Corporation (Retired); Director, Combustion Engineering, Inc., New York, New York

HENDRIK W. BODE, Professor, Division of Engineering and Applied Physics, Harvard University, Cambridge, Massachusetts

THOMAS H. BURBANK, Vice President, Edison Electric Institute, New York, New York

ROBERT CITRON, Director, Center for Short-Lived Phenomena, Smithsonian Institution, Cambridge, Massachusetts

BRUCE S. OLD, Senior Vice President, Arthur D. Little, Inc., Cambridge, Massachusetts

E. L. QUARANTELLI, Professor, Department of Sociology, and Co-Director, Disaster Research Center, The Ohio State University, Columbus, Ohio

CHARLES E. REED, Senior Vice President, General Electric Company, New York, New York

RALPH H. TURNER, Professor, Department of Sociology, University of California, Los Angeles, California

CHARLES E. FRITZ, *Executive Secretary*

PANEL ON THE PUBLIC POLICY IMPLICATIONS OF EARTHQUAKE PREDICTION

RALPH H. TURNER, *Chairman,* Professor, Department of Sociology, University of California, Los Angeles, California

CLARENCE ALLEN, *ex officio,*[*] Department of Geology and Geophysics, California Institute of Technology, Pasadena, California

WILLIAM A. ANDERSON, Professor, Department of Sociology, Arizona State University, Tempe, Arizona

JAMES M. BROWN, Professor, The National Law Center, The George Washington University, Washington, D.C.

JEROME W. MILLIMAN, Professor, Department of Economics, University of Florida, Gainesville, Florida

E. L. QUARANTELLI, Professor, Department of Sociology, and Co-Director, Disaster Research Center, The Ohio State University, Columbus, Ohio

[*]Dr. Allen is Chairman of the NRC Committee on Seismology's Panel on Earthquake Prediction.

ROBERT H. SIMPSON, Research Professor, Department of Environmental Sciences, University of Virginia, Charlottesville, Virginia

H. R. TEMPLE, JR., †U.S. Army War College, Carlisle Barracks, Pennsylvania

Staff, Advisory Committee on Emergency Planning

CHARLES E. FRITZ, *Executive Secretary*
SARAH OSGOOD BROOKS, *Editorial Assistant*

Liaison Representatives to Panel on the
Public Policy Implications of Earthquake Prediction

JOSEPH W. BERG, JR., Executive Secretary, Division of Earth Sciences, National Research Council, Washington, D.C.

C. MARTIN DUKE, Professor, School of Engineering and Applied Science, University of California, Los Angeles, California

J. EUGENE HAAS, Professor of Sociology, Institute of Behavioral Sciences, University of Colorado, Boulder, Colorado

ROBERT M. HAMILTON, Chief, Office of Earthquake Studies, U.S. Geological Survey, National Center, Reston, Virginia

HOWARD C. KUNREUTHER, Professor of Decision Sciences, The Wharton School, University of Pennsylvania, Philadelphia, Pennsylvania

JAMES F. LANDER, Deputy Director, National Geophysical and Solar Terrestrial Data Center, National Oceanic and Atmospheric Administration, Boulder, Colorado

ARNOLD J. MELTSNER, Associate Professor, Graduate School of Public Policy, University of California, Berkeley, California

UGO MORELLI, Program Officer, Preparedness Division, Federal Disaster Assistance Administration, Department of Housing and Urban Development, Washington, D.C.

RICHARD PARK, Technical Director, Advisory Committee on Civil Defense, National Research Council/National Academy of Sciences, Washington, D.C.

ROBERT E. SCHNABEL, Chief, Preparedness Division, Federal Disaster Assistance Administration, Department of Housing and Urban Development, Washington, D.C.

KARL V. STEINBRUGGE, Manager, Earthquake Department, Insurance Services Office, San Francisco, California

†Colonel Temple is the former Director, State of California Office of Emergency Services.

CHARLES C. THIEL, JR., Deputy Director, Division of Advanced Environmental Research and Technology, RANN, National Science Foundation, Washington, D.C.

ROBERT E. WALLACE, Chief Scientist, Office of Earthquake Studies, U.S. Geological Survey National Center, Menlo Park, California

Contents

1	Conclusions and Recommendations	1
2	Earthquakes and Earthquake Prediction	20
3	Earthquake Hazard and Constructive Response to Prediction	35
4	Issuing Predictions and Warnings	47
5	Economic Implications of Earthquake Prediction	67
6	Legal Implications of Earthquake Prediction	81
7	The Problem of Equity	96
8	Political Implications of Earthquake Prediction	105
9	Some Potentially Constructive Responses to Earthquake Warning	118

1 Conclusions and Recommendations

The conclusions and recommendations that follow are distilled from the entire report. What they announce in summary form is examined and explained more fully in subsequent chapters. For convenience, the conclusions and recommendations are grouped under six headings. We first consider the prospect that prediction will be a useful tool in the arsenal of weapons for mitigating the disastrous effects of earthquakes. We then examine some of the contingencies that will affect all aspects of planning for constructive use of the advance warning provided by earthquake predictions. The description of a constructive program of response to earthquake prediction is divided into four main phases, making up the remainder of the six headings in the chapter. First is the release of predictions and the issuance of warnings. Second come hazard-reduction measures—steps that can be taken following the prediction to lessen the impact of the quake on life, property, and social order. Third is the readying of emergency services to perform their post-disaster tasks of rescue and rehabilitation more effectively than they could have done without advance warning. And fourth are steps to cope with responses to the prediction that may be counterproductive toward the economic and social foundations of community life.

Under each heading we present "conclusions" that summarize our findings and "recommendations" that state in capsule form a few of the most significant steps we believe are warranted by the conclusions. We emphasize recommendations for action. Being painfully aware of how little we understand the events that will be set in motion by a prediction or how to deal constructively with them, we also offer a few carefully selected recommendations for research. We single out only the most important areas in which the lack of information and understanding is a serious obstacle to planning for the constructive use of earthquake prediction.

PREDICTION AS A TOOL IN EARTHQUAKE MITIGATION

CONCLUSIONS AND RECOMMENDATIONS FOR ACTION

Earthquake prediction is still in a research stage; networks of instrumentation needed for dependable prediction are inadequate except perhaps in one small area of California; and historical baseline data against which to detect the premonitory signs of a large earthquake are not yet available. But theory and experience are advanced enough to justify confidence that an expanding prediction capability may be imminent. By prediction we mean the specification of place, time, and magnitude of earthquakes within sufficiently narrow limits to permit short-term and long-term actions to save life and property. The precise nature and circumstances of prediction are difficult to foretell at the present time, and the way individuals and communities will respond is even less foreseeable. By applying what we know about responses to other disasters and other warnings and drawing upon the disciplines of sociology, economics, political science, and legal studies, we can offer some tentative guidance to those who must cope with the first scientifically credible prediction of a potentially destructive earthquake.

Much will be learned from experience with the first few predictions of serious earthquakes. Guidelines must be applied flexibly and will surely be modified on the basis of each experience. In the short run, the public priority assigned to earthquake prediction should not be reduced because of counterproductive community responses to a specific prediction. We hope that judicious and early planning will ensure a constructive response to the very first prediction of a serious earthquake. But the human capacity to learn from earlier mistakes should not be underestimated. As communities find ways to "normalize" earthquake prediction, the benefits and costs will be quite different from what they are when prediction is encountered without prior experience, and modified guidelines will be needed.

Experience with prediction of minor earthquakes will undoubtedly accumulate rapidly and will be important in perfecting predictive theory and technique. But the concern of public policy is primarily with earthquakes of potentially destructive magnitude. Consequently, our conclusions and recommendations deal with earthquakes of magnitude 6 and above.

There will be disadvantages as well as advantages to earthquake prediction. Under the worst combination of an inaccurate prediction and an inappropriate public response, the prediction and quake together might even be more costly than an unpredicted quake would have been. But it is our considered judgment that earthquake prediction *can* be a means for substantially reducing the losses from earthquakes if appropriate social, economic, engineering, and legal actions are taken prior to the quake. Even in the case of a false alarm, some of the costs of a well-planned hazard-reduction program will contribute to the long-term seismic safety of the community.

The potential benefits from prediction are likely to be greater in saving lives and lessening physical injury than in reducing property losses. There is a real danger that preoccupation with immediate economic costs of such hazard-reduction measures as demolishing unsafe structures and protecting community lifelines could prevent people from undertaking or supporting programs that might save thousands of lives.

Recommendation 1 The highest priority in responding to earthquake prediction should be assigned to saving lives, with secondary attention to minimizing social and economic disruption and property loss, provided the costs of specific measures are within the limits that society is willing to accept. (See Chapter 2, p. 24; Chapter 3, pp. 35-45; and Chapter 9, pp. 118-120, and 123.)

Judged by the potential for saving lives, continued investment in perfecting earthquake prediction merits priority as a government activity. At the present stage in the development of prediction, a higher priority should still be placed on research into earthquake prediction than on the establishment of operational systems for prediction.

Both the probabilistic nature of earthquake prediction and the prospect that the predicted quake will be preceded by an uncertain time window (i.e., a period of days, weeks, or even months) create difficulties in determining the appropriate responses to a prediction. Selective evacuation, the shutdown of vulnerable lifelines, and similar life-saving steps would usually be impracticable for prolonged periods. Costly hazard-reduction measures such as demolishing buildings would be uneconomical for predicted earthquakes with either a relatively low probability of occurrence or a low level of confidence in the prediction. A few years' advance warning combined with assurance that the exact time of occurrence could be pinpointed as the event neared would afford the greatest opportunity for saving both lives and property. Accordingly, emphasis in earthquake-prediction research should be placed on efforts to narrow the predictive time window and identify immediately precursory signs.

Perhaps the development of a highly accurate prediction capability will change the emphasis currently placed by decision makers on such adjustments as building resistance and land-use management; however, until such a capability is developed, the achievement of the maximum potential benefit from earthquake prediction will require its use in conjunction with the full range of hazard-reduction measures. The prospects for developing a constructive and life-saving response to prediction in an area where many structures are already quake-resistant are more favorable than they are in an area where practically all structures are vulnerable. We should not wait for a prediction to begin practicing informed land-use management and to adopt building codes designed to encourage the construction of earthquake-resistant structures.

Recommendation 2 Prediction should be used in conjunction with a complete program of earthquake-hazard reduction, and not as a substitute for any of the procedures in current use. (See Chapter 2, p. 24; Chapter 3, pp. 35 and 41–45; and Chapter 9, pp. 119 and 124.)

NEEDED RESEARCH

The need for more systematic empirical data on responses to earthquakes and to earthquake predictions should already be obvious. Inferences about the impact of earthquake prediction on social, political, economic, and legal systems often depend on the use of tenuous analogies to other types of human crisis and warning. There is much to be learned from carefully conceived research at the present time, but the greatest advancement in understanding will result from carefully planned monitoring of responses to actual predictions of moderate and major earthquakes.

Research Recommendation 1 High priority should be assigned to developing a standby anticipatory research capability to be utilized as future earthquake predictions are issued. The standby research plan should include comprehensive examination of the social, economic, legal, and political effects of the prediction and of the actual quake.

Baseline data are as necessary for assessing the social, economic, and political effects of earthquake prediction as for recognizing the premonitory physical signs of an earthquake. Geophysical monitoring networks now being established by the United States Geological Survey (USGS) provide an excellent opportunity for coordinating the observation of physical and socioeconomic data.

Research Recommendation 2 Socioeconomic monitoring should be established concurrently with geophysical monitoring in order to develop baseline data and methodology, to serve as a standard for measuring the social, political, and economic impact of earthquake prediction, and to refine techniques that can be applied to other regions as the geophysical monitoring networks are expanded.

Accumulation of understanding about the public policy implications of earthquake prediction will be a slow process because of the infrequency of serious earthquakes in the United States, unless investigators take advantage of experience in other countries. Furthermore, application of earthquake prediction and warning in developing countries where earthquake risk is high could have a significant life-saving potential.

Research Recommendation 3 Continuing investigation should be made of experiences in utilizing earthquake prediction in countries such as Japan, the Soviet Union, and China, and of the effects of introducing prediction technology in other countries, such as developing nations where earthquake risk is high.

DISASTER-PREPAREDNESS PLANNING FOR EARTHQUAKES

CONCLUSIONS AND RECOMMENDATIONS FOR ACTION

Earthquakes of destructive magnitude in the United States typically recur in a given region at intervals of years or decades. Years may pass without a destructive quake in the nation, and there is no recurrent annual "earthquake season." Earthquake protection derives primarily from the incorporation of knowledge about earthquakes into building codes, land-use management and control programs, and other similar continuing activities. For these reasons the responsibilities for preparing for predictions and responding to them should generally be assigned to agencies having broad concerns with community and economic planning and with disaster planning and response. An agency established exclusively to cope with earthquake prediction would surely stagnate and suffer reduced funding during an interval of years without a substantial earthquake crisis. A specialized body, such as the newly formed California Earthquake Commission, can be important in maintaining active attention to all aspects of earthquake hazard, but implementation is still accomplished through more broadly based agencies.

Earthquake predictions will probably differ substantially from warnings of other natural disasters because current theories suggest that long periods of advance warning will precede serious quakes. The traditional response to disaster forecasting has been to activate a program of emergency mobilization under the direction of civil defense agencies, the police, and other units concerned with public safety. But with months or years of advance warning the problem is chiefly one of long-range planning rather than short-term response. Although emergency forces will benefit from the opportunity to plan for a predicted event and must be integrally involved in all response planning, the most significant activities in response to a long-term prediction will fall within the usual province of departments of planning, building and safety, engineering and public works, and the like. A substantial reorientation of thinking and authority in these matters will be essential.

Recommendation 3 The primary responsibility for planning and responding to earthquake predictions should be assigned to federal, state, local, and private agencies having broad concern for community and economic planning and for disaster preparedness and response, rather than to newly formed agencies established especially to deal with earthquake prediction and warning or to agencies concerned primarily with emergency response. (See Chapter 8, p. 106, and Chapter 9, pp. 123, 125, and 126.)

Dealing effectively with predictions of earthquakes will require a well-orchestrated effort involving federal, state, and local governments, professional associations, business and labor leaders, and coordinated planning across many local jurisdictional boundaries. Development and execution of a plan suited to local circumstances must be the responsibility of the several local jurisdictions. But the accumulation of experience and technical knowledge necessary for developing a plan is beyond the capacity of local governments, and federal and state governments must therefore share in this responsibility. For example, authentication of predictions will require review by a qualified panel of experts, and the governors of states have a major responsibility for issuing and implementing warnings. Just as a disaster-stricken community must draw upon state and national resources for recovery and reconstruction, there must be a similar use of ouside resources during the prediction interval.

Because we lack exact precedents and analogies, all phases of earthquake prediction and response will be plagued initially by legal uncertainties. If we are to make constructive use of the prediction capability, these uncertainties must be clarified as quickly as possible, with legislation when necessary. A determination must be made of whether long-term prediction establishes a state of emergency justifying the exercise of extraordinary police powers. A determination must also be made of whether exercise of emergency police powers in response to long-term

Conclusions and Recommendations

prediction carries with it an obligation to compensate those whose property is taken.

Recommendation 4 As an essential feature of advance planning, legal determinations and clarifying legislation should be sought to minimize the legal ambiguities that otherwise will hamper officials in making constructive response to earthquake prediction. (See Chapter 6, pp. 88 and 94.)

The most effective mechanism for instituting federal, state, and local collaboration and protecting officials from legal jeopardy probably is to adapt to the circumstances of earthquake prediction the present post-disaster procedure of declaring that an emergency exists under the provisions of the Disaster Relief Act of 1974. Legislation may be needed to provide assurance that the terms of PL 93-288 can be applied on the basis of an appropriately authenticated prediction and the determination that many lives and a substantial amount of property are at risk in the area. Such a designation would then activate various kinds of technical and financial assistance. With the activation of certain critical prediction-responsive programs being mandatory rather than discretionary upon the declaration of an emergency, local officials could feel more confident that decisions made in the public interest would be made without undue risk of legal or political liability.

Recommendation 5 Legal inquiry should be undertaken to clarify what powers for responding to earthquake predictions now exist under the Disaster Relief Act of 1974 (PL 93-288) and what further powers might be necessary. Any deficiency or uncertainty regarding application to the emergency created by prediction of a potentially destructive earthquake should be promptly corrected by new legislation. (See Chapter 6, p. 94, and Chapter 9, p. 138.)

In all aspects of planning and response to earthquake predictions, the interests of different segments of the community are likely to be unequally served. In the preoccupation with general community welfare and effective promotion of self-interest by well-organized groups, the disproportionate costs and risks borne by less powerful and less well-organized groups are easily overlooked.

Recommendation 6 A public agency should be assigned the responsibility of (a) identifying groups of people most likely to need special assistance in the event of an earthquake or to suffer disproportionate loss and disruption when an earthquake is predicted, (b) developing a plan to offset, insofar as is practicable, the inequitable costs and suffering attendant on both the quake and the prediction, (c) monitoring events after the prediction from the point of view of equity, and (d) helping unorganized population segments to recognize how the earthquake prediction affects their interests. (See Chapter 4, p. 52; Chapter 7; Chapter 8, pp. 114–115; and Chapter 9, p. 129.)

NEEDED RESEARCH

Legal problems are so complex and so crucial to the selection of effective strategies in responding to earthquake prediction that wide-ranging study is needed.

Research Recommendation 4 A comprehensive study should be launched on the legal problems likely to be encountered as earthquake-prediction capabilities develop. Preparation of a compendium of federal and state laws pertaining to earthquake prediction and earthquake-mitigation measures would be a useful beginning.

Within our complex structure of government and private agencies it is difficult to pinpoint responsibilities in connection with earthquake prediction; coordination among various agencies may not always be easy.

Research Recommendation 5 A comprehensive investigation should be conducted on the division of function and responsibility among the various levels of government and the interrelationships among government and private agencies whose efforts must be coordinated in connection with earthquake prediction and hazard mitigation.

PREDICTION AND WARNING

CONCLUSIONS AND RECOMMENDATIONS FOR ACTION

It is useful in developing public policy to make a clear distinction between *prediction* and *warning*. *Prediction* is a statement indicating that an earthquake of a specified magnitude will probably occur at a specified location and time, based on scientific analysis of observed facts. A prediction is strictly information; it says nothing about how people should respond and takes no account of the consequences that may follow from the issuance of the prediction. Issuance and assessment of predictions are strictly technical matters to be debated only on technical grounds.

A *warning*, on the other hand, is a declaration that normal life routines should be revised for a time. Warnings are issued because of a judgment that public welfare will be served thereby. Warnings are normally based on predictions or other types of technical information, but not all predictions will be followed by warnings. Issuance and assessment of warnings are peculiarly the responsibility of public officials acting in the interests of the people they represent.

In many instances the record of premonitory signs will not come together at a single moment so as to justify prediction, but will accumulate incrementally from early signs to late refinements in the prediction. The interests of some groups with investments in the predicted danger area will be served by taking defensive action based on fairly early indications and doing so before the information is generally known. Other groups' interests may be served by suppression and denial of predictions. Public officials may prefer that predictions not be issued until they are ready to issue warnings. The play of these forces on scientists could deprive some people of information when they need it most and could undermine the public credibility of the prediction process.

Many people lack the background to understand the meaning of prediction, especially when it is stated in probabilistic terms; they could also have difficulty distinguishing between a scientifically authenticated prediction and one with no scientific validity. Hence it is important that there be cooperation among scientists, public officials, and the communication media to provide understandable and unsensational interpretations of reported predictions. In addition, a continuing informational program is needed to convey the knowledge of scientists concerning earthquake mechanisms and prediction to public officials and citizens.

Recommendation 7 Predictions should be developed, assessed, and issued to the public by scientists rather than by political officials. Procedures must be developed to ensure the free and timely flow of information concerning predictions to all segments of the public. Legislation may be required to assure that information that an earthquake will occur at a given location and time will not be withheld from general knowledge to the advantage of special interests. (See Chapter 2, p. 32–33; Chapter 4, p. 57; Chapter 5, pp. 70 and 77; Chapter 7, p. 98; Chapter 8, pp. 107 and 109; and Chapter 9, pp. 127 and 129.)

In the immediate future, predictions may originate from a variety of public and private sources and may range in validity from well founded to irresponsible. Public officials, the media, and the general public will require the advice of a disinterested group of scientists in distinguishing valid from invalid predictions. Governors in some states may establish their own boards of experts, but the need for a federally based group will not be lessened by such action.

Recommendation 8 A designated federal agency should establish a group of governmental and nongovernmental scientists who can be called upon to evaluate specific earthquake predictions. The responsibility for establishing this group should not be vested in any agency that is involved in the technical pursuit of earthquake prediction. This agency should also maintain a public record of all published predictions. (See Chapter 4, pp. 58, 61, and 62; Chapter 6, p. 82; and Chapter 8, p. 107.)

At present the responsibility for issuing warnings in case of an earthquake prediction is dangerously undefined. In some instances governors of affected states may assume the responsibility in collaboration with chief executives of the principal local jurisdictions concerned. In other instances state and local officials may assume that some federal agency will take the responsibility. Initially the governors or the federal agency chief will have to exercise considerable discretion in determining when to issue a warning and whether to secure independent evaluations. It is urgent that these ambiguities be resolved at once. As the theory and practice of earthquake prediction are perfected and experience is accumulated, standards should be developed at the federal level to serve as guidelines in issuing warnings.

Recommendation 9 A designated federal agency should confer promptly with governors of the principal earthquake-prone states or their representatives to clarify the respective responsibilities at each level of government and to establish procedures for issuing earthquake warnings. (See Chapter 4, pp. 59 and 63–64; and Chapter 8, p. 109.)

Public officials may be deterred from issuing warnings by the unjustified fear of panic, by the fear that a prediction judged to be false will cause people to disregard the next warning altogether, by pressure from local interests who fear economic loss from the disruption of normal community life, and from fear of the political consequences of the warning. But leaders will eventually be forced to issue warnings, and undue delay can only diminish the trust in public officials that is essential in preparing for the quake.

Experience with other disasters suggests that warnings may be widely discounted and ignored and that inaction rather than panic flight will be the most common response among the general public. Especially in case of long-term predictions, the remoteness of the threat will impart a sense of unreality. The absence of external signs through which people can confirm the threat with their own senses creates a special problem of credibility. Cooperation of the communication media will be important in helping people to visualize concretely the laboratories, the seismographic networks, and the panoply of instruments and devices through which predictions are developed. Outlining concrete response plans

Conclusions and Recommendations

should help to add a sense of reality to the warning as well as to forestall some disorganized or disruptive responses. The development of constructive ways in which citizens and groups can participate actively in the preparedness program should also help to bolster public credence.

Recommendation 10 A warning should be issued by elected officials promptly after a credible prediction of a potentially destructive earthquake has been authenticated. A warning should include a frank assessment of the prediction, noting the possibilities for error, information on the types and extent of damage that the earthquake could cause, a statement concerning plans being developed to prepare for the quake, and advice concerning appropriate action to be taken by individuals and organizations. (See Chapter 4, pp. 49, 59, and 63; and Chapter 8, p. 107.)

Warnings, like predictions, must be periodically reviewed, reaffirmed, and revised. In making warnings effective, public officials will require a continuous flow of information about the beliefs, attitudes, and actions of the public in response to the warning. Warnings will either not be received or not be understood by some segments of the population. Special efforts must be devoted to ensuring that all segments receive warnings promptly and that they fully understand their import.

Recommendation 11 A designated federal agency should establish mechanisms for monitoring public understanding, credence, and response at all stages of the prediction-warning-earthquake sequence, and for making this information available promptly to responsible public officials. (See Chapter 2, p. 29; Chapter 4, pp. 48–49; Chapter 7, pp. 98 and 101, and Chapter 9, pp. 128–129.)

Recommendation 12 Careful attention should be paid to the problems of communicating to segments of the population that might otherwise receive only last-minute warnings. These segments include such groups as foreign-speaking minorities, the physically handicapped, tourists, and the socially isolated. (See Chapter 4, p. 52; Chapter 7, pp. 98–100; and Chapter 9, p. 129.)

NEEDED RESEARCH

The future success of any earthquake-prediction and earthquake-warning system depends largely on whether public officials, business executives, and the populace assign high credibility to earthquake predictions and warnings. We have too little understanding of how the usual difficulties in securing public acceptance of disaster warnings will be intensified by such unusual features of earthquake prediction as the following: potentially long lead times (months or years) before the predicted occurrence of a destructive quake; the public's lack of experience with severe quakes because of their infrequent occurrence; the absence of external signs by which the public can confirm that an earthquake will shortly occur, could have occurred, or still may occur; and the likelihood of false alarms and unpredicted quakes.

Research Recommendation 6 Circumstances influencing the credibility of earthquake predictions and warnings, and techniques for improving their credibility, need more careful study.

Research Recommendation 7 Research is needed on how people process information regarding low-probability disasters and how this processing changes when a prediction alters the probability. It is important to gain more understanding of how people establish acceptable levels of risk in such instances.

Although there is a fairly extensive literature on how people regard tornadoes, hurricanes, floods, and other natural disasters, less is known about popular conceptions of earthquakes and earthquake predictions. In planning earthquake-hazard-reduction measures, public officials and business leaders must know how people view earthquakes, because their perceptions will strongly influence their responses.

Research Recommendation 8 Popular perceptions and understandings of earthquakes and earthquake prediction should be investigated, comparing populations in different earthquake-prone regions of the United States and also comparing people who have had no previous experience with earthquakes with those who have experienced severe or minor quakes.

HAZARD-REDUCTION MEASURES

CONCLUSIONS AND RECOMMENDATIONS FOR ACTION

The prospect of weeks, months, or years of advance warning greatly enlarges the protective action that can be taken before a quake, but it also creates the possibility that the prediction itself will produce unemployment, community disruption, loss of income, and declines in property values. A comprehensive prediction–response program will include three components: a program of hazard reduction to minimize the loss of life and property and community disruption when the quake occurs; a program of readying emergency services to deal with the postquake problems that are likely to occur; and a program to control potentially disruptive consequences of the prediction. Hazard reduction offers the greatest challenge and opportunity of the three.

Conclusions and Recommendations

The prospect of substantially reducing the earthquake hazard on the basis of a prediction will be greatest when there is a plan in readiness before a prediction is made and when the plan is part of a continuing program of hazard reduction. Where standards for earthquake-resistant construction are already in existence and enforced, where some continuing identification of safe and unsafe structures is maintained, where land-use planning has systematically taken seismic risk into account, the response to earthquake prediction will largely be a selective acceleration of existing programs. Problems will be of manageable dimensions, and the citizenry can be prepared to accept the prediction and the inconveniences attendant on the implementation of hazard-reduction measures.

Recommendation 13 As part of a complete and continuing earthquake-mitigation program, each earthquake-vulnerable community should develop a hazard-reduction program, involving both public and private agencies, to be put into effect in case of an earthquake warning. A designated federal agency should establish a central clearinghouse to provide the necessary hazard-reduction information and technical assistance to states, which in turn will aid communities in developing their plans and in implementing them. (See Chapter 3, pp. 41–44; Chapter 4, pp. 63; Chapter 9, pp. 119–126, 131–137, and 141.)

Unlike floods, hurricanes, and tornadoes, earthquakes would seldom be lethal were it not for the structures humans build that cannot withstand violent earth movement. Except for danger from tsunamis, landslides, and mass fires triggered by the quake, an earthquake is more frightening than dangerous for most people in the quake area who are at a safe distance from vulnerable buildings and other hazardous structures. Most deaths occur when structures or parts of structures collapse on people. Much of the property loss and disruption comes from this effect and from such side effects as fire and the rupture of lifelines. The prospect of death and destruction from collapsing dams may be exceedingly great in some future earthquakes. Accordingly, hazard-reduction strategy centers on dealing with earthquake-vulnerable structures.

Each situation will be unique, and no standard set of hazard-reduction measures can be offered for all cases. The period of advance warning, length of the prediction time window, concentration of population, economic costs, legal constraints, and credence placed in the prediction will all affect the possibilities for action. With several years of advance warning, the principal activity could be to reinforce or demolish and selectively rebuild vulnerable structures. In a few instances it may be possible to relocate structures away from the most vulnerable locations. Land-use planning and management and structural design and maintenance programs must work in concert.

With shorter lead times and as the period of danger approaches, more attention will be given to such actions as vacating vulnerable buildings, evacuating dangerous locations, lowering the water level in dams, closing down atomic power plants if necessary, discontinuing use of vulnerable gas lines, taking precautions against fire, closing off vulnerable roadways and other transportation routes, and restricting traffic in selected areas. Massive evacuation of the population will seldom be practicable, though it may be the only realistic course of action where nearly all structures are vulnerable and the time of occurrence for the quake can be pinpointed. Mobile homes and tents might be used to house some activities temporarily. Under some circumstances the example of the Chinese, who sleep and work outdoors when an earthquake is predicted, might be followed in the United States.

Recommendation 14 Each threatened community should examine the applicability of each of the following major kinds of hazard-reduction measures: (a) evacuating limited areas and vacating dangerous structures; (b) accelerating structural design and maintenance programs; (c) employing land-use planning and management powers in relation to the predicted locale of the quake; (d) protecting essential natural gas lines and other community lifelines; (e) dealing with such possible hazards as nuclear plants, vulnerable dams, highly flammable structures and natural cover, and facilities involving the risk of explosion or the release of dangerous chemicals. (See Chapter 3, pp. 42–45, and Chapter 9, pp. 119–126 and 131–136.)

Any hazard-reduction program will be expensive, though with effective planning the costs should be offset by reduced property loss and economic disruption from the actual quake. The longer the period of advance warning, the greater the possibilities for absorbing much of the cost regionally. Low-cost federal loans and urban-redevelopment funds might suffice in part. When lead time is less, or where most structures are vulnerable, considerable outside subsidy will be required. It is accepted policy for federal and state governments and private agencies to provide massive financial and other assistance to a community *after* disaster has struck. A crucial step toward effective hazard reduction is recognition of the principle that much of this assistance should be available to a community *before* the disaster strikes, when there is a well-authenticated prediction.

Recommendation 15 It should be accepted policy on the part of public and private agencies that a considerable part of the financial assistance normally available to a community after an earthquake should be made available as needed for hazard-reduction measures taken in response to an authenticated prediction of a potentially destructive earthquake. New legislation should be enacted as required to achieve this end, taking into account the example of such existing legislation as PL 93-288, the Disaster Relief Act of 1974, especially Title IV, Section 417 of that Act on "Fire Suppression Grants" (see Recommendation 5). (See Chapter 5, pp. 70–71; Chapter 6, p. 94; and Chapter 8, pp. 111–112.)

Insurance has been proposed as a way of spreading losses and providing incentives, through rate differentials, for investing in earthquake-resistant construction. However, once earthquake predictions are made, then insurance may not be marketable in its current form. Companies will be reluctant to issue new policies in areas where the quake is predicted, and most individuals will have little interest in purchasing insurance in areas where quakes are *not* forecast. A thorough study is needed of the potential role of insurance as an approach to the problem of hazard reduction and of the political and economic implications of alternatives to the current system of voluntary earthquake insurance. For example, should "compulsory insurance" be issued in the form of a property tax and, if so, what role should federal, state, and local governments play in providing funds for recovery following a catastrophic earthquake? (See Chapter 5, pp. 74–76, and Chapter 6, pp. 93–94.)

NEEDED RESEARCH

When viewed in the abstract, many of the measures that seem most promising as parts of a hazard-reduction program in response to an earthquake prediction may prove difficult to implement or ineffective because of various social, political, economic, psychological, and legal considerations. Evacuation of the population from selected areas and the use of earthquake insurance to spread risk are especially important measures about which our present knowledge is inadequate for making sound policy decisions.

Research Recommendation 9 Intensive study is needed on the feasibility of implementing the hazard-reduction measures suggested in Recommendation 13 and on their probable effectiveness.

Research Recommendation 10 A thorough study is needed of the potential role of insurance in the problem of hazard reduction and of the political and economic implications of alternatives to the current system of voluntary earthquake insurance.

Assessment of the merits of various hazard-reduction measures depends upon having satisfactory ways to estimate the losses from future earthquakes. Present methods have severe limitations that impair their usefulness for decision makers in the public and private sectors. Few rigorous data are available on the benefits and costs associated with each of the major hazard-reduction measures.

Research Recommendation 11 Research should be conducted on refining the theory and method of estimating losses from future earthquakes and on comparing the benefits and costs of various alternative hazard-reduction measures.

Hazard-reduction programs will be implemented in settings marked by a complex interaction among public and private organizations and groups. An adequate assessment of the merits of different hazard-reduction measures can be attained only when this interaction is more fully understood.

Research Recommendation 12 Several prototype economic models for earthquake-prone regions should be developed for estimating the dynamic interactions among the public sector, businesses, and households, assuming alternative earthquake-warning sequences.

READYING EMERGENCY SERVICES

CONCLUSIONS AND RECOMMENDATIONS FOR ACTION

There is much accumulated experience with emergency planning at local, state, and federal levels. Earthquakes may not have been covered specifically by emergency planning in many communities where the risk is substantial because they are infrequent events. When emergency planning for earthquakes has been completed, it is generally based on the assumption that the quake will occur without advance warning. The advent of earthquake prediction provides a new and significant opportunity for emergency services to be placed in readiness before the quake to perform their postdisaster tasks of rescue, relief, and rehabilitation with augmented effectiveness. Both public and private agencies should be able to use the period between warning and quake to prepare their personnel and facilities for the response to the earthquake when it comes.

Recommendation 16 Emergency plans in earthquake-vulnerable areas should be revised to include programs for readying emergency services in the interval between warning and quake. (See Chapter 3, p. 44, and Chapter 9, pp. 131–137.)

This phase of earthquake preparation is most easily understandable to the layman and is most suitable for large-scale active citizen involvement. Much can be learned from the early experience with civil defense units. Long-term standby civilian organization is not recommended, since activities soon lose their meaning in the absence of imminent threat. But emergency plans should provide for activation of citizen involvement directly upon issuance of a warning, with intensified and broadened involvement as the predicted time approaches. If these programs are also used to impart a sophisticated understanding of the nature of prediction and the broader problems of preparing for an earthquake, they will serve at least three important purposes: to upgrade the effectiveness of the community's response when the quake occurs; to enhance the credibility of the prediction by involving people in readily understandable action; and to augment public support for some of the less popular but essential measures in preparing the community for the earthquake.

Recommendation 17 Emergency plans should include programs for broad and active citizen involvement in preparing for the earthquake. (See Chapter 4, p. 59; Chapter 8, pp. 109–110; and Chapter 9, pp. 128–129.)

DEALING WITH COUNTERPRODUCTIVE CONSEQUENCES OF PREDICTION

CONCLUSIONS AND RECOMMENDATIONS FOR ACTION

We know less of what to expect in counterproductive consequences from the prediction and have less basis for making action recommendations for this than for any other aspect of the problem. Evidence from other threatening situations suggests that most inhabitants of an area will attempt to continue life as usual. However, the foundation of the regional or local economy may be significantly influenced. Regional and national business and financial associations may decide to limit mortgages, insurance, and investment in the threatened area. There may be outmigration of sizable numbers of people, and the tourist trade may be adversely affected. If some or all of these conditions continue throughout a long pre-earthquake period, secondary effects such as rising unemployment, falling property values, and reduced community tax revenue will ensue. The latter developments would quickly become the focus of political concern and recrimination.

Recommendation 18 Upon issuance of an earthquake warning, a joint governmental and private-sector commission should be established to monitor the economy in the threatened area to ensure early detection of changes and to make recommendations to government, business, and labor organizations as needed. Representatives of insurance and investment organizations should be included and should play an integral part in the work of the commission. (See Chapter 3, p. 44; Chapter 5, p. 76; and Chapter 9, p. 138.)

Underlying all policy discussions will be the general question of whether to sustain the community or to allow and encourage an orderly outflow of capital and population. Intensive economic studies of the probable costs and benefits of the two approaches in a few carefully selected earthquake-vulnerable communities are needed now. But sustaining the community in its present form is likely to be the more politically popular course of action. Whichever course is followed, costs of the transition (unemployment, relocation costs, and loss of rental and other income) will fall disproportionately on some groups of people. Outside financial assistance will be required to ease these costs.

If businesses and workers are to be relocated, a federal or regional authority will have to be assigned responsibility for the program. In the more likely event that the effort is to sustain the community, a federal program will be required to guarantee loans and insurance settlements, extend eligibility for unemployment payments, and generally underwrite the local economy. Funds introduced into the community for the hazard-reduction program will offset weakening of the local economy to varying degrees, depending on a variety of circumstances.

Recommendation 19 In the event of a credible earthquake prediction, policy makers must continuously weigh the relative merits of sustaining the economy in the threatened area at its prewarning level or of encouraging some orderly outflow of capital. Economic subsidies may be required either to sustain the economy or to protect groups of people who would otherwise suffer undue hardship as a consequence of economic dislocation resulting from the prediction and warning. (See Chapter 3, p. 44; Chapter 5, pp. 69–76; and Chapter 7, p. 97–98.)

Public awareness of an earthquake-prediction capability will probably be accompanied by an increase in the number of businesses and individuals offering services related to earthquake mitigation to the public. Many of these services will be valuable adjuncts to publicly provided services. But standards and regulations will sometimes be required to protect the public. In extreme cases, the unscrupulous may even disseminate false information to encourage panic selling or to encourage homeowners to undertake unnecessary or inappropriate reconstruction.

Conclusions and Recommendations 19

Recommendation 20 Consideration should be given to the development of standards to govern the practices of businesses and individuals offering services related to earthquake mitigation to the public. (See Chapter 5, pp. 74–78; Chapter 6, p. 92; and Chapter 7, pp. 103–104.)

NEEDED RESEARCH

The fear of economic dislocation in the community following an earthquake prediction and the fear that national corporations may respond in such a way as to weaken the local economy may be well founded or quite unjustified. Some research into these questions has been started, but public officials need much more information than we now have.

Research Recommendation 13 Research is needed on the probable decisions affecting the economy of the threatened area made by both local and national business and financial leaders and the various economic interactions that are likely to result from these decisions.

Research Recommendation 14 The likely effects of earthquake predictions on how various kinds of markets process information and discount changes in the size and timing of losses should be studied in depth. Special attention should be focused on markets for securities (private and public), land markets, financial institutions, insurance practices, metropolitan and local public finance, and problems of financing and maintaining public utility operation.

2 Earthquakes and Earthquake Prediction

EARTHQUAKES IN THE UNITED STATES

Seventy million people throughout the United States live with a significant risk to their lives and property from earthquakes. Another 115 million are exposed to a less significant, but not negligible, seismic risk. Only 8 percent of Americans can safely ignore the earthquake hazard. But most Americans occupy, use, or are served by constructed facilities that were not designed to resist earthquakes and that could collapse in a quake with major losses of life and property. Even in California many facilities are not up to reasonable standards of safety from seismic disturbance.

In the history of the United States there have been approximately 1,300 deaths and 4 billion then-current dollars worth of property damage resulting from earthquakes. A few of the United States earthquakes are described in Table 1. While more than half of the deaths occurred in San Francisco in 1906, and most of the total dollar losses occurred in three quakes—San Francisco (1906), Alaska (1964), and San Fernando (1971)—future losses of life and property will probably be much greater because many more people and more extensive facilities are now concentrated in vulnerable cities. For example, a great earthquake in metropoli-

TABLE 1 Representative Earthquakes

Earthquake and Year	Richter Magnitude	Maximum Modified Mercalli Intensity	Surface Faulting Length, Miles	Number of Deaths	Property Loss, Millions of Then-Current Dollars
San Fernando, Calif., 1971	6.4	IX	8	65	550
Alaska, 1964	8.4	X	450	125	310
Montana, 1959	7.1	X	14	28	11
Kern County, Calif., 1952	7.7	XI	14	12	60
Long Beach, Calif., 1933	6.3	IX	Epicenter in ocean	102	50

tan Los Angeles or San Francisco could take as many as 15,000 lives and do 25 billion dollars worth of property damage.[1,2,3]

Earthquakes come in many sizes, usually reported in terms of Richter *magnitude,* which is a measure of the vibrational energy released. The magnitudes of five representative earthquakes are given in Table 1 for illustrative purposes. The magnitude of the Alaska earthquake was the largest ever recorded in the United States, while quakes equal in magnitude to the recent San Fernando disaster are frequent throughout the seismically active regions of the world. The scale is such that an earthquake of given magnitude releases about thirty times the vibrational energy of an earthquake one unit less on the scale.

Before instrumentation was widely available, only the observed effects were reported. More recently, these effects are grouped into intensity levels according to established scales such as the Modified Mercalli Intensity Scale presently in use in the United States. While a given earthquake's magnitude is expressed by a specific number, its intensity varies at different locations. When a single intensity value is given, it usually refers to the maximum intensity, as is the case in Table 1 and Figure 1.

[1]C. M. Duke and D. F. Moran, "Earthquakes and City Lifelines," *The San Fernando Earthquake of February 9, 1971, and Public Policy,* Special Subcommittee of the Joint Committee on Seismic Safety, California Legislature (Sacramento: California Legislature, 1972), pp. 53–72.

[2]National Oceanic and Atmospheric Administration, U.S. Department of Commerce, *A Study of Earthquake Losses in the Los Angeles, California, Area* (Washington, D.C.: U.S. Government Printing Office, 1973), pp. 165–169.

[3]National Oceanic and Atmospheric Administration, U.S. Department of Commerce, *A Study of Earthquake Losses in the San Francisco Bay Area* (Washington, D.C.: U.S. Government Printing Office, 1972), pp. 117–125.

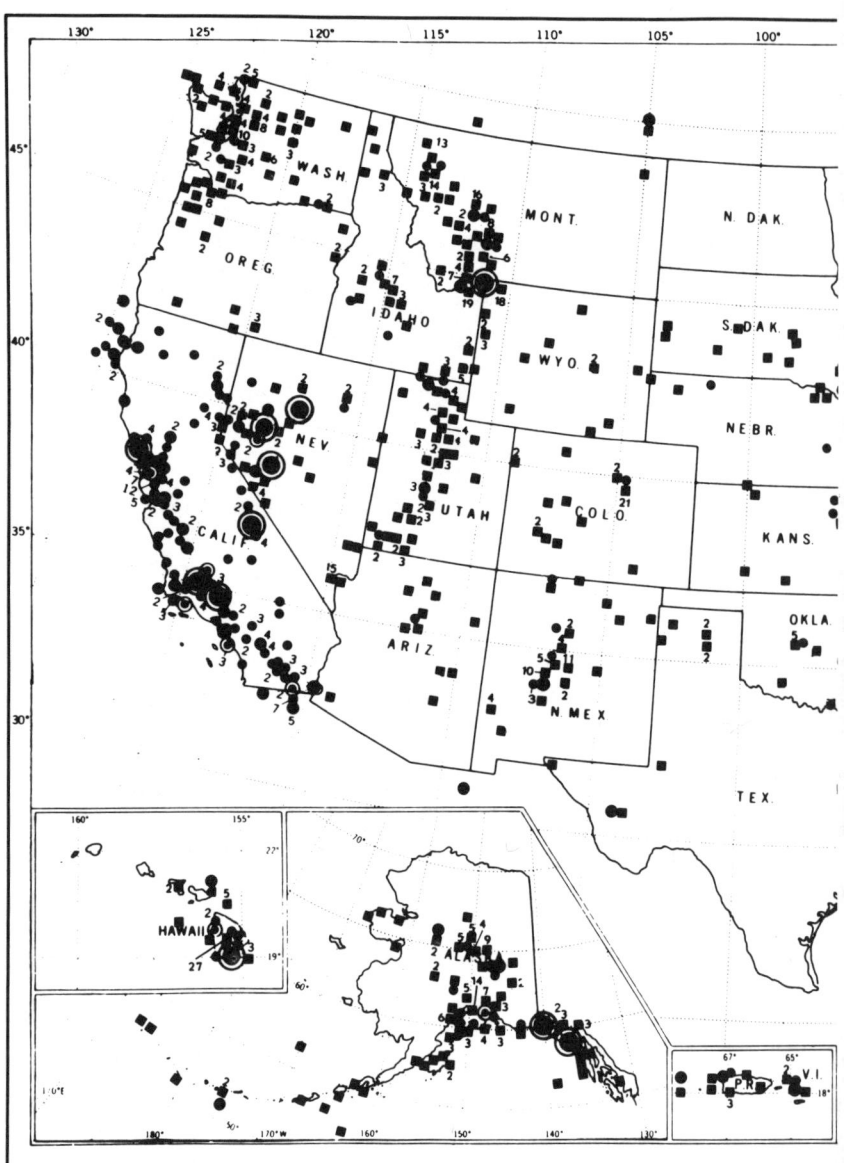

FIGURE 1 Earthquakes of Modified Mercalli Intensity V and above in the United States through 1970.

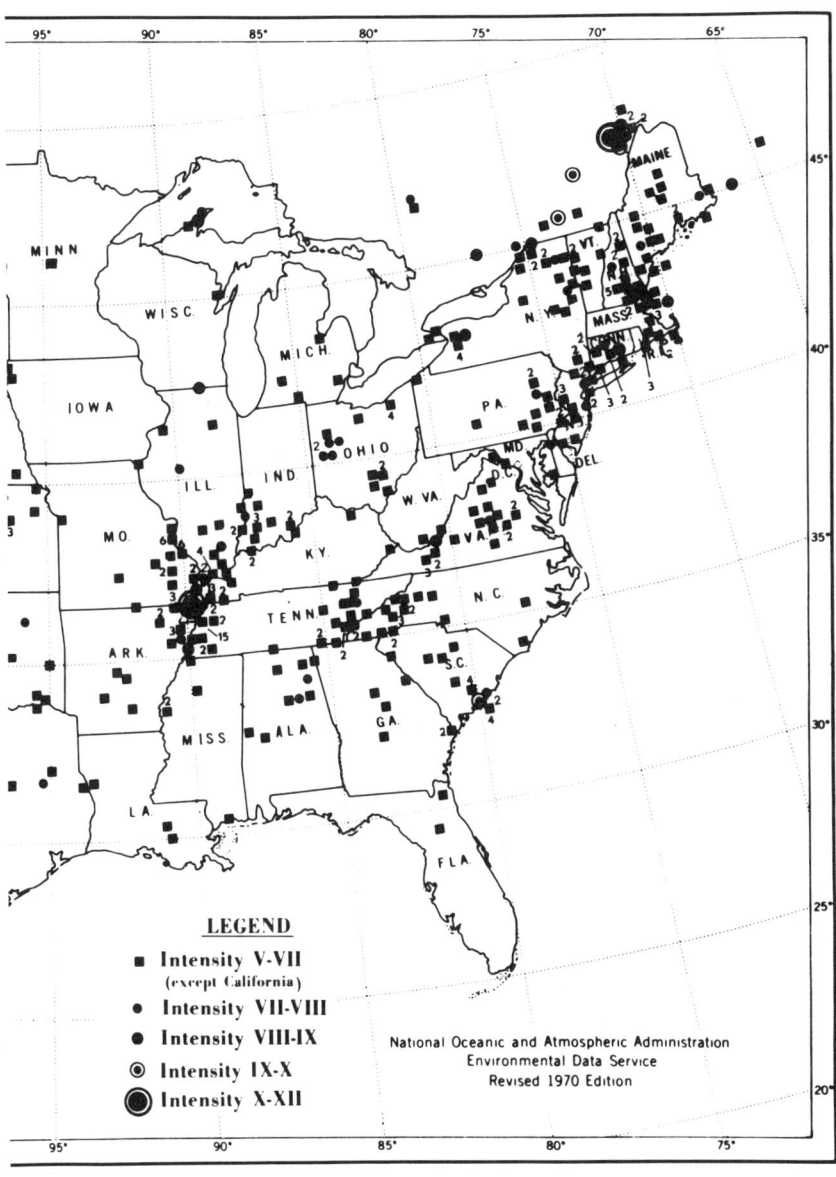

Fortunately, the larger magnitudes and intensities are experienced much less often than the smaller ones. Intensity X or greater has been experienced only thirteen times in recorded U.S. history. The locations of earthquakes throughout the United States (Figure 1) show that California and Alaska have no monopoly on seismic activity. The Mississippi Valley, the Rocky Mountain states, New England, and portions of the southeastern seaboard have had considerable experience with earthquakes.

EARTHQUAKE PREDICTION

Earthquakes have often been viewed as unique among natural disasters because they occur suddenly and without advance warning. Nevertheless, we have long identified regions where the likelihood of earthquakes is high, as contrasted with regions where earthquakes are considered unlikely. The frequently mentioned prospect of one or more major quakes in the southern California section of the San Andreas fault within a century and a predicted recurrence of a 1906 type of earthquake in the San Francisco Bay region are well-known examples of forecasting that is nonspecific as to time and place of occurrence. Similar assumptions using previous experience with earthquakes and geologic evidence form the bases for seismic-risk mapping. These understandings can be—and sometimes are—reflected in building codes and in other long-term precautions to reduce the earthquake hazard.

Within the past 5 years, many seismologists have become convinced that a new development is imminent, namely, the *prediction* of earthquakes. By prediction seismologists mean that the place, time, and magnitude of the quake are specified, within fairly close limits, with the consequence that accelerated planning to save life and property is possible. Established methods for identifying high-risk areas depend largely on the past incidence of quakes and the mapping of fault structures. The new methods rely primarily on premonitory signs, such as changing physical properties of rocks under stress and surface tilting, that occur in advance of a quake. Prediction capability does not lessen the importance of other approaches to earthquake mitigation, but it adds one potentially telling weapon to the arsenal.

The opportunity to devise means for saving life and property through constructive long- and short-term actions and the necessity for coping with potentially counterproductive responses to earthquake predictions constitute the social challenge of earthquake prediction.

Efforts to develop constructive public policy should be based on a realistic assessment of the prospects for prediction and on informed judgment concerning the nature of prediction. Seismologists have not yet reached consensus on these matters. Hence the following statement is tentative and will need revision from time to time.

STATUS AND PROSPECTS OF EARTHQUAKE PREDICTION

PRESENT STATUS OF PREDICTION

Earthquake prediction is in a stage of research and development. No operational system for prediction yet exists. Within the research framework, several physical systems or models appear promising for explaining changes that have been noted before earthquakes, and each model suggests possibly ten or more measurable physical, chemical, electrical, and other changes that may serve as precursory evidence of an earthquake. No one of these models or possible measurements is as yet clearly the best or only one to employ in an operational prediction system; very likely a combination will be needed. But observation of the same changes prior to earthquakes in widely separated parts of the world and successful prediction of a few minor earthquakes give confidence that an operational earthquake-prediction system will become feasible.

Research in the field and laboratory is refining the understanding of existing models, and new models are evolving. Some instruments for recording certain precursory changes are operational, some are in the developmental stage, and still others are only concepts at this time. No nets of instruments are as yet designed primarily to serve as operational earthquake-prediction systems. Only limited areas in California have what might be called a dense network of any kind. However, those research networks that are currently being used to monitor precursory signs very likely will suffice for limited types of predictions of nondestructive quakes.

A widespread, operational network of instruments monitoring several phenomena that will have been well established as valid earthquake precursors must await some years of additional research and the buildup of the network. The timetable for such an operational network rests both on successful research breakthroughs—which are inherently unpredictable—and on funding and deployment of the operational network.

PREDICTING SERIOUS QUAKES

Although the study of small earthquakes contributes to the understanding of seismology, larger earthquakes of magnitude 5 or 6 and above are the principal concern for public policy. Earthquakes smaller than this pose very little threat to life, property, or social order. Because the precursors for larger earthquakes are believed to develop over a period of years, long periods of observation will be required before they can be predicted with a high degree of confidence. Furthermore, potentially destructive quakes occur so infrequently in the United States that several decades may be required to secure enough experience to perfect the technique of predicting them. However, even these larger quakes may show some precursory signs shortly before their occurrence, making possible some short-term hazard-reduction responses.

The potential for significant earthquake prediction is not limited to the western United States. Indeed, the first successful prediction of a small earthquake in the United States took place in the state of New York.[4] But for areas of the United States in which earthquakes of destructive magnitude are extremely infrequent, where the mechanisms of earthquakes are less well understood, and where, as yet, there are no dense networks of instrumentation comparable to those existing in California, prediction is still in the indefinite future.

CHARACTERISTICS OF EARTHQUAKE PREDICTION

A tentative characterization of earthquake prediction as it may develop in the next 10 to 30 years is the essential starting point for developing public policy. At present, empirical observations are leading the way in prediction although theories that explain the observations have been developed. The reader should refer to the sources listed at the end of this chapter for more technical discussions of earthquake prediction from the point of view of physical science and engineering.

SPECIFICITY OF PREDICTION

Current thinking leads us to expect that under favorable conditions and with sufficient experience seismologists will be able to issue reasonably confident predictions that indicate the approximate place, time, and magnitude of anticipated quakes. For earthquakes that are severe enough to subject the community or region to substantial risk, the premonitory signs should be observable months or years before the event. Consequently both the possibilities for hazard- reduction activity and the potential for community disruption in response to an earthquake warning are much greater than we are accustomed to in the case of flood,

[4]Christopher H. Scholz, Lynn R. Sykes, and Yash P. Aggarwal, "Earthquake Prediction: A Physical Basis," *Science*, 181 (August 31, 1973), 803–810.

Earthquakes and Earthquake Prediction

hurricane, and tornado warnings. Experience gained from predicting other types of disaster will not provide adequate guidance to us in planning for earthquake prediction.

MAGNITUDE AND ADVANCE WARNING

The lead time between premonitory signs and the earthquake should increase with the magnitude of the quake, according to existing observations. Minor quakes will have lead times of a few hours, days, or weeks. Many of these quakes will not even be felt by most inhabitants, and damage, if any, will be minimal. Moderate earthquakes should allow periods for advance warning measured in weeks or months. Some of these earthquakes will be widely felt and will do substantial damage, especially to inadequately built structures and to unsecured objects. Warning signs of major earthquakes could range from several months to several years in advance of the event. Lead times as long as 10 to 40 years have been projected hypothetically. These and the larger "moderate" events are the quakes that pose important threats to life and property. They are the chief concern for public policy. These relatively long periods of advance warning as well as the specificity of predictions will be possible only with an adequate record of prior seismic observations and a dense network of monitoring stations in the affected areas. In the absence of these prerequisites, predictions will often be less specific and will provide much shorter lead times.

INCREMENTAL NATURE OF WARNINGS

Particularly in the case of moderate and major quakes, the assurance that an earthquake is actually on the way and the specificity of the prediction with respect to time and magnitude will probably improve incrementally over an extended period of time. Under favorable conditions, initial signs will alert seismologists to the possibility of an impending quake, and the extent of the area in which anomalies occur will provide some hints of the magnitude. Persistence and intensification of the initial signs, and consistency among different signs, will progressively strengthen confidence that a quake is in the offing and will supply a firmer basis for estimating the time of occurrence and the magnitude.

Because the nature of the prediction sequence will probably be incremental, it is misleading to think of issuing the prediction at some strategically selected moment or withholding it until it can be issued with maximal confidence and specificity. For earthquakes with potentially serious consequences, public officials must be prepared to cope with predictive communications that develop by increments from initially vague and uncertain statements over a considerable period of time.

PINPOINTING THE TIME OF OCCURRENCE

A mature earthquake prediction will identify a span of time within which the earthquake is expected to occur—e.g., between January 15 and February 15. The length of this *time window* will increase with the magnitude of the quake (at least until more is learned about the signs immediately preceding moderate and major quakes). In the case of major quakes, the span is likely to be from a month to a year or more. Seismologists are hopeful that new understanding of signs will eventually allow them to recognize immediate precursors a few minutes, hours, or days before the event. That capability has not yet been demonstrated, however. Thus we must assume that the time window for pinpointing the occurrence of potentially damaging quakes will range from a few weeks to a year or more. This conclusion is of crucial importance when considering the feasibility of such short-term remedies as evacuation, closing down essential services, and maintaining key personnel on round-the-clock alert status.

ABSENCE OF EXTERNAL SIGNS

Unlike floods, hurricanes, and tornadoes, earthquakes are preceded by no external signs through which the public can make their own informal confirmations of the prediction or identify the moment of occurrence. If a scientifically based prediction specifies a time window of a day, a month, or a year's duration for occurrence of the quake, the individual cannot watch for visible signs telling when to evacuate or take other last-minute precautions, as would typically be done in the case of other natural disasters. Nor can one seek confirmation of the scientific prediction in direct sensory evidence (looking for a funnel-shaped cloud or watching for increased rainfall) or from news reports of publicly observable developments nearby.

If a predicted quake fails to appear on schedule, the public will have no visible evidence to confirm that an earthquake *could* have occurred, or that it still may occur. If scientifically detectable stresses are accumulating at a site, eventually there should be an earthquake. Unlike a hurricane or a tornado, it does not go somewhere else. But again there will be no visible signs by which the public confirms the scientist's confidence that the eventual likelihood of a quake is increased rather than lessened when it is "past due."

Earthquakes and Earthquake Prediction 29

These circumstances make earthquakes distinctive among predicted natural disasters in the extent to which public response will depend exclusively on the faith people are willing to place in scientific prediction. In case of error it also leaves the scientist in an exceptionally vulnerable position, unable to call on any but his own scientific observations to justify his erroneous prediction.

FREQUENCY OF MINOR QUAKES

Minor quakes are frequent occurrences in California and Nevada. If many of these small quakes are predicted, residents in such earthquake-prone regions will soon become accustomed to the idea of earthquake prediction and perhaps develop some confidence in it. However, their attitudes toward earthquake prediction will be formed on the basis of events having only trivial effects. While experience with minor quakes is important for perfecting predictive technique, it will not prepare officials or the public for dealing with the long periods of advance warning, the extended time windows, the threat of counterproductive response, and the serious consequences of inaction following prediction of a potentially damaging earthquake.

INFREQUENCY OF DAMAGING QUAKES

In contrast to minor tremors, damaging quakes occur so infrequently in any one location that every prediction of such an earthquake is likely to be the first such experience for most of the inhabitants of the affected area and for most of the personnel charged with preparing for the event. Hence the accumulation of direct experience with earthquakes by personnel in a local area cannot provide the basis for constructive action in response to warnings of an impending major earthquake. This observation is important when considering how to divide responsibility for dealing with earthquake predictions between local and national agencies, whether to establish new agencies for dealing with earthquake predictions or to assign these responsibilities to agencies that already deal with other matters of public safety and welfare, and how to approach the problem of educating the public to understand and respond constructively to earthquake predictions.

PROBABILITY AND CREDIBILITY IN EARTHQUAKE PREDICTIONS

In case of major—and even moderate—earthquakes, prediction sets the stage for both community and private responses that can mean great expense and inconvenience for large numbers of people. Consequently, false alarms can be quite costly and destructive of human values—many times more so than false alarms concerning floods, hurricanes, or tornadoes. But for the period of at least a generation, seismologists foresee no predictions that can be announced with absolute certainty. After a few years of experience, it should be possible to assign probability estimates to most predictions when they are made. Hence public policy must be developed on the assumption that occasional disruptive and expensive false alarms are unavoidable.

The complementary problem is whether some major and moderate earthquakes will occur without being predicted. Seismologists have not yet verified that all quakes are preceded by the same premonitory signs, though many believe that certain premonitory signs should appear for all except quakes induced by such special circumstances as the filling of artificial lakes and volcanic activity. Furthermore, earthquakes can be predicted only where sufficiently intensive networks of monitoring stations are installed and in use, and where the history of recorded observation supplies a baseline from which to detect premonitory anomalies. At present only a few restricted areas are blanketed to this extent, and baseline data everywhere are insufficient for major quakes. Hence, for the present, officials and the public must assume that some major or moderate earthquakes may occur without advance notice.

As public awareness of prediction capability increases, so will the frequency of nonscientific predictions issued by seers, pseudoscientists, and others. In some segments of the public the difference between these low-credibility predictions and the highly credible but probabilistic scientific predictions will not be readily understood. Consequently, the efforts to prove and disparage unscientific predictions may weaken belief in scientific predictions, and the statements of probability may be interpreted as admissions of dubious credibility.

The New Madrid earthquakes of 1811–1812 and the Charleston, South Carolina, earthquake of 1886 are dramatic reminders that destructive earthquakes do occur outside the more highly seismic zones of the western United States. Recurrence times for major earthquakes in the eastern United States are believed to be much longer than in California and Alaska. Little is known about the mechanism of these earthquakes as there are no surface expressions of the faults that caused these or most other eastern earthquakes. As our recorded history is short with respect to the cycle time, destructive earthquakes may occur in areas not now recognized as significantly active seismically. Because of the more efficient transmission of seismic waves in the eastern United States, the area affected by a destructive earthquake of comparable energy release will be several times greater in the east than in the west. These differences will pose special problems in monitoring, predicting, and responding to predictions outside the western states.

NEGATIVE PREDICTION AND IMMUNIZATION

Some observers have expressed the hope that seismologists may someday be able to give assurances that *no* significant earthquake will occur in designated locations during some specified number of years. If that were possible, such *negative predictions* would be of great help to citizens and public officials in planning for the future. At the present time, however, the uncertainties besetting negative prediction are even greater than those attending positive predictions. It is premature at this time to include the possibility of dependable negative prediction in the contingencies for public policy.

When an earthquake prediction is issued, public officials, private investors, and individual residents and merchants will be anxious to know whether they can plan for a period of increased security after the event. Even in the absence of any basis in fact, popular belief that "lightning never strikes in the same place twice" is prevalent. Earthquakes are normally followed by aftershocks, often of destructive magnitude. But beyond the period of aftershocks, recurrence of a severe quake within a half century has been fairly rare in the recorded history of the United States. Since major quakes normally release energy that accumulated over a period of many years, there is hope that seismologists may learn to distinguish those instances in which a major quake "immunizes" a locale against recurrence for a generation or more. But for the present, neither the evidence nor the understanding of seismic phenomena will justify such assurances.

THE INEVITABILITY OF EARTHQUAKE PREDICTIONS

In light of the uncertainties of earthquake prediction and the possibilities of costly responses to false predictions, some people have asked whether we should not give up the effort to develop a prediction capability and concentrate our limited public resources in other paths to human betterment. Others have made the more modest proposal for a moratorium on public release of earthquake predictions for several years until highly reliable and precise predictions are assured. Such views, we believe, reflect a profound misunderstanding of the situation in which we find ourselves.

Earthquake prediction is a fact at the present time, and its refinement is an inevitable by-product of research on the nature of earthquake causation and process. Research into the nature of earth movements, which is necessary if we are to design more earthquake-resistant buildings, also produces many of the data used in making predictions. Refinement of earthquake-prediction theory and technology advances hand in hand with progress in understanding earthquakes as physical phenomena. By minimizing attention to earthquake prediction we may only slow the process of rendering predictions precise and dependable. The only way to stop further developments would be to cut off all further study of earthquakes, which would be highly destructive of human welfare.

Attempts to suppress information concerning premonitory signs would certainly fail—as they should. Once the public recognizes that the capability exists, the demand for predictions will be insistent. Recent discussion of the advisability of predicting earthquakes has already led to newspaper editorials condemning earth scientists for allegedly seeking to suppress information to which the public is entitled. The demand for predictions, the long period between the time when premonitory signs first appear and the occurrence of potentially destructive quakes, and the inevitable dissemination of some if not all of the data upon which predictions are based all converge to make the suppression of "leaks" an insuperable task, as well as an undesirable objective. Furthermore, there are as many leading seismologists outside of government employment as within it who have access to the theory and technology at hand. It would be exceedingly difficult to control the work of all these independent scientists. There is no way to monopolize prediction capability; there is no way to prevent detection of the signs on which predictions are based; and there is no way to prevent dissemination of predictions.

Finally, like access to "inside" information in the stock market, restricted access to earthquake prediction gives insiders distinct advantages over outsiders. Since property values are likely to be affected by earthquake predictions, individuals with advance knowledge stand to gain at the expense of others. If prediction takes place through inadvertence or is the exclusive province of privately employed seismologists, the probability of unequal gain and loss is maximized. Only by accepting prediction as an inescapable public responsibility can this source of potential inequity and exploitation be minimized.

With earthquake prediction an inescapable reality, the only realistic questions are whether to have precise and reliable forecasting or imprecise and unreliable forecasting, and whether to turn our energies toward making the most constructive possible use of this capability.

THE PROSPECT

For at least the immediate future we must anticipate the frequent issuance of predictions from diverse public and private sources, based on evidence of varying adequacy. In many instances highly responsible scientists will properly issue predictions in spite of low confidence levels rather than withhold information that *might* save lives. This state of affairs will almost surely outlast the tenure of most officials currently holding responsible public offices. The most realistic and useful approach in developing public policy now is to plan for an extended period of steady advancement in the art of prediction. Especially in the case of serious earthquakes, false alarms and missed predictions are to be expected, and most predictions will be issued with explicit reference to a substantial possibility of error.

In spite of the uncertainties, public officials will not be able to disregard the infrequent predictions of potentially destructive earthquakes. Suppression of information is neither desirable nor possible. As we shall see in the next chapter, many lives could be lost needlessly if appropriate actions are not taken. When a potentially destructive earthquake is predicted, public officials must assess and interpret the announcement for the public and exercise leadership in developing an appropriate community response. With many lives at stake, the formulation of public policy cannot wait for the refinement and perfection of an earthquake prediction capability.

SELECTED REFERENCES

Coffman, Jerry L., and Carl A. von Hake (ed.). *Earthquake History of the United States.* National Oceanic and Atmospheric Administration, U.S. Department of Commerce, Publication 41-1, Revised edition. Washington, D.C.: U.S. Government Printing Office, 1973.

Duke, C. M., and D. F. Moran. "Earthquakes and City Lifelines," *The San Fernando Earthquake of February 9, 1971, and Public Policy.* Special Subcommittee of the Joint Committee on Seismic Safety, California Legislature. Sacramento: California Legislature, 1972.

Earthquake Engineering Research Institute. *Managua, Nicaragua, Earthquake of December 23, 1972.* Conference Proceedings, San Francisco, California, November 29 and 30, 1973. 2 vols. Oakland: Earthquake Engineering Research Institute, 1973.

Greensfelder, Roger W. "Progress in Earthquake Prediction," *California Geology, 27 (August 1974), 188–189.*

Kisslinger, Carl. "Earthquake Prediction," *Physics Today,* 27 (March 1974), 36–42.

National Oceanic and Atmospheric Administration, U.S. Department of Commerce. *A Study of Earthquake Losses in the Los Angeles, California Area.* Washington, D.C.: U.S. Government Printing Office, 1973.

National Oceanic and Atmospheric Administration, U.S. Department of Commerce. *A Study of Earthquake Losses in the San Francisco Bay Area.* Washington, D.C.: U.S. Government Printing Office, 1972.

National Oceanic and Atmospheric Administration, U.S. Department of Commerce. *San Fernando, California, Earthquake of February 9, 1971.* 3 vols. Washington, D.C.: U.S. Government Printing Office, 1973.

Office of Emergency Preparedness, Executive Office of the President. *Disaster Preparedness.* 3 vols. Washington, D.C.: U.S. Government Printing Office, 1972.

Press, Frank. "Earthquake Prediction," *Scientific American,* 232 (May 1975), 14–23.

Press, Frank. "Plate Tectonics and Earthquake Prediction: Contrasting Approaches in China and the United States," *Bulletin of the American Academy of Arts and Sciences,* 28 (May 1975), 14–27.

Richter, Charles F. *Elementary Seismology.* San Francisco: W. H. Freeman and Company, 1958.

Scholz, Christopher H., Lynn R. Sykes, and Yash P. Aggarwal. "Earthquake Prediction: A Physical Basis," *Science,* 181 (August 31, 1973), 803–810.

Steinbrugge, Karl V. "Earthquake Damage and Structural Performance in the United States," *Earthquake Engineering,* R. L. Wiegel (ed.). Englewood Cliffs, N.J.: Prentice-Hall, 1970.

3 Earthquake Hazard and Constructive Response to Prediction

The formulation of public policy concerning earthquake prediction naturally begins with the question: What could we do to limit the death, injury, disruption, and property loss from an earthquake if we had a fairly good indication in advance as to the time and place of its occurrence and its approximate magnitude? The answer depends first on identifying the specific hazards of earthquakes, and then on considering what might be done about each of them. In this chapter we shall briefly outline the hazards and then indicate the main elements that might enter into a constructive public response to prediction of a potentially destructive earthquake.

THE EFFECTS OF EARTHQUAKES

Strong earthquakes manifest themselves on the earth's surface in several ways that are disruptive to human works and activities:

Violent shaking, resulting in
  Vibrations
  Avalanches
  Soil liquefaction
  Lurching
  Seiches (oscillations and fluctuating levels in bodies of water)
Tectonic movement, expressed as
  Regional uplift and subsidence

Fault breaks reaching the earth's surface
Tsunamis (seismic sea waves)

Table 1 (p. 21) contains cases illustrative of all these manifestations. Violent shaking was present in all of them, and shaking dominated the scene in the quakes at San Fernando, Kern County, and Long Beach. Tectonic movements were prominent features of all the quakes except Long Beach. The tsunami that accompanied the Alaska quake invaded many waterfront areas in western Canada, Washington, Hawaii, and Oregon, as well as California. A lake-creating avalanche accompanied the earthquake in Montana.

The primary effects of earthquakes are death, injury, and suffering; damage to systems and structures; and disruption of normal activities. Most deaths and injuries can be attributed to

Collapsing structures
Falling debris, such as bricks and glass
Tsunamis inundating communities
Avalanches engulfing communities
Floods from collapsed dams or levees
Earthquake-induced fires
Release of toxic, chemically reactive, and radioactive materials

In the Long Beach quake of 1933, most of the 102 fatalities were due to the collapse of non-earthquake-resistant buildings. There are numerous examples of deaths in the tens of thousands from collapsing non-earthquake-resistant structures in earthquakes in southern Europe, Latin America, the Middle East, and the Far East: More than 75,000 died in Messina, Italy, in 1908; 30,000 in Chile in 1939; 11,000 in Iran in 1968; and more than 180,000 in China in 1920.[1]

The tsunami that wiped out several seacoast and bayshore communities was responsible for most of the deaths in the 1964 Alaska quake. Even greater damage and more fatalities resulted from the Chilean quake of 1960 in which the tsunami generated in the Pacific, after killing some 4,000 Chileans, went on to cause fatalities in Hawaii, and additional fatalities and property damage over 22 hours later in Japan. A 1946 quake in the Aleutians triggered a tsunami that killed 163 people in Hawaii, but none in Alaska.

An avalanche above the Madison River was responsible for 17 of the

---

[1] Office of Emergency Preparedness, Executive Office of the President, *Disaster Preparedness,* Vol. III (Washington, D.C.: U.S. Government Printing Office, 1972), pp. 71–87.

20 deaths in the Montana earthquake of 1959. The epicenter was in a sparsely populated area. The Peru quake of 1970 triggered an avalanche in the Andes which completely engulfed some 20,000 people in two towns some nine miles from the avalanche source.

Dam failures leading to sudden release of reservoir water and consequent deaths and damage have occurred several times under nonearthquake conditions, but to date fatalities and damage from this cause have not been directly associated with earthquakes in the United States. The Sheffield Dam in Santa Barbara, California, failed completely in the 1925 earthquake, but apparently it did not cause deaths or major downstream damage. Nevertheless, there are existing situations that could lead to such calamities. For example, the Lower San Fernando Dam in the San Fernando earthquake came perilously close to flooding its downstream area, which is inhabited by 80,000 people.

Fires induced by earthquakes should be considered in context with both structure and lifeline (i.e., utilities and transportation systems) damage. More than 40 percent of the 143,000 casualties in the Tokyo–Yokohama earthquake of 1923 resulted from fires following the quake. Fortunately, major conflagrations following earthquakes have not occurred in the United States since 1906, but there are many possibilities of such occurrences. One element of earthquake fire hazard is the high-rise building, whose upper floors cannot be reached by truck-mounted equipment and whose elevators are likely to be inoperable following an earthquake. Furthermore, the pipelines supplying the water needed for firefighting are highly vulnerable to earthquake damage.

An earthquake could generate risks for surrounding populations if a nuclear reactor were damaged. Additional risks would also occur if the effectiveness of normal measures taken to protect radioactive material in storage or in transit were weakened.

DAMAGE TO BUILDINGS

Damage to buildings depends strongly on the type of construction and the location. Unreinforced masonry buildings constitute the greatest existing seismic hazard, in contrast to buildings constructed so that they contain some degree of earthquake resistance. This point was strongly made in the Kern County, California, quake of 1952, which affected Bakersfield and its environs. In that earthquake many of the standard old-style buildings of unreinforced brick masonry suffered extensive damage, while those of earthquake-resistant construction (e.g., grouted reinforced brick masonry) fared much better. This contrast was again demonstrated in San Fernando in 1971, and again in the disastrous Managua quake of 1972, even though some buildings of modern design did experience severe damage.

Legions of similar old non-earthquake-resistant buildings are still in use in practically all seismic regions of the world. In California seismic-resistant building regulations were adopted after the Long Beach earthquake of 1933, but few of the older buildings have been brought up to standard. Los Angeles County alone contains approximately 40,000 of the older buildings, some more than six stories high. Probably 15 to 20 percent of the population either live or work in such unsafe buildings. Long Beach, California, is the only known city with a vigorous program of replacing or strengthening the pre-1933 buildings or limiting their occupancy rates.

While the California problem with old buildings is serious, it must be emphasized that California, through enforcement of modern codes for new construction and the gradual obsolescence of some of the old construction, is moving steadily toward a condition of relative seismic safety. On the other hand, seismic hazard receives much less attention in seismic areas outside of California and Alaska. In particular, one may look at Memphis, Tennessee, Boston, Massachusetts, and Charleston, South Carolina, where major quakes have occurred in historic time. These cities contain very little construction that is specifically designed for earthquake resistance. Memphis and Boston have begun to face the problem recently and apparently will somewhat enhance the seismic safety of their new construction, at least for major structures and works. But in view of the fact that the seismic risks in those cities are not so readily apparent as they are in Los Angeles, San Francisco, and other western cities that frequently experience quakes, it would be economically and politically unreasonable to expect them to adopt the same rigorous standards. Because the eastern cities are less likely to experience minor earthquakes, they will remain much more vulnerable to catastrophic damage from the occurrence of future major quakes.

In any discussion of seismic safety, interest naturally gravitates to the high-rise buildings because of the hundreds or thousands of occupants of each building whose lives may be at stake. Only two persons have been killed in contemporary tall buildings during earthquakes in the United States. A number of buildings of up to 16 stories that had been designed and built according to modern earthquake engineering state of the art survived the 1972 Managua quake, though some sustained major structural damage. This was the first such test since the 1971 San Fernando earthquake, where structural damage was experienced by several contemporary 6–14-story hospital and office buildings in the more strongly shaken area. The tall buildings of modern design in downtown Los Angeles, away from the epicenter, experienced only superficial damage. On the other hand, in the Caracas, Venezuela, earthquake of 1967, there were several accordion-type collapses of 10-13-story buildings that had been designed for some earthquake resistance, but not to the degree of resistance characterizing the modern high-rise buildings in Managua and San Fernando.

DAMAGE TO LIFELINES

Every city has lifelines that provide for the supply and flow of people, goods, information, energy, and water by means of the transportation, communication, energy, and water systems. In general, a lifeline is a network within which there are sources, major transmission lines, storage, and a distribution or collection system. Lifelines are often public utilities. Each has a terminus usually outside the city, and an extensive network of contact or distribution points inside. For example, the natural gas supply of Los Angeles is piped in from Texas and the San Joaquin Valley of California and crosses numerous fault lines.

Each type of lifeline has its own characteristic design and operational features and its own special vulnerabilities to earthquakes. The low level of earthquake-engineering practice relative to city lifelines was shown by the 1971 San Fernando quake. During that quake freeway bridges failed, aqueducts broke, there were electric power outages, gas transmission line ruptures, and near total collapse of a major earth dam. Comparable calamities befell Managua, Nicaragua, in 1972. Fires following the Managua quake, as well as the 1906 San Francisco quake, could not be extinguished or controlled because of loss of water. Severe harbor damage resulted from earthquakes in southern Chile in 1960 and Niigata, Japan, in 1964.

Existing facilities present problems different from those of facilities now under design. The problems are analogous to those of strengthening or demolishing non-earthquake-resistant buildings. Given a significantly higher state of the art of lifeline earthquake engineering, it would take perhaps 100 years for the existing facilities to be brought up to the new standards through normal obsolescence and replacement.

Summarizing the situation regarding damage to lifelines, the engineering state of the art is inferior to that for buildings, even in California. The property losses resulting from earthquake damage to lifelines have been of the same order of magnitude as for buildings. However, the collective risk to life probably is less than from damaged buildings.

DISRUPTION OF NORMAL ACTIVITIES

In a major earthquake both damage to buildings and lifelines and the community effort required to respond to casualties and destruction significantly disrupt traditional individual and group activities in all spheres of life—from work to recreation, from religious worship to banking services. An earthquake does more than wreck buildings and sever lifelines; if it does not interrupt the rhythms and patterns of community and social life, then it at least puts a strain on them. Because stores and factories are often closed, not only are some people temporarily unemployed, but necessary goods and services often cannot be obtained in the usual ways when they are wanted, and various governmental agencies do not receive their normal tax revenues. Because schools may be closed and most formal recreational activities curtailed, children are forced back onto their families. For varying degrees of time, breadwinners are not able to perform their usual provider roles, and religious, welfare, and relief organizations and agencies have to augment and extend their usual services and develop completely new programs for the newly unemployed and otherwise disadvantaged. Government units have to drop or curtail some of their traditional services, such as street maintenance, refuse collection, and enforcement of clean air standards, and have to develop new ways of dealing with the convergence of people, materials, and information on the impacted area, the problem of possible profiteering, and the coordination of efforts with state, regional, and federal agencies with which they have had no previous contact. Private business concerns will have similar problems.[2]

While there is little reason to think that most victims of an earthquake will become apathetic, or that impacted communities will degenerate into a state of chaos, the disruptions will have both individual and organizational consequences. Among the emotional stresses engendered will be anxiety, various psychosomatic reactions, and frustrations over sheer problems of living. Community agencies will not collapse into anarchy,

---

[2]For further information on the kinds of disruptions that earthquakes may occasion see Committee on the Alaska Earthquake, National Research Council, *The Great Alaska Earthquake of 1964: Human Ecology* (Washington, D.C.: National Academy of Sciences, 1970); Daniel Yutzy, William Anderson, and Russell Dynes, *Community Priorities in the Anchorage, Alaska, Earthquake, 1964* (Columbus, Ohio: Disaster Research Center, Monograph No. 4, 1969); David S. Adams, *Emergency Actions and Disaster Reactions: An Analysis of the Anchorage Public Works Department in the 1964 Alaska Earthquake* (Columbus, Ohio: Disaster Research Center, Monograph No. 5, 1969); and William Anderson, *Disaster and Organizational Change: A Study of the Long-Term Consequences in Anchorage of the 1964 Alaska Earthquake* (Columbus, Ohio: Disaster Research Center, Monograph No. 6, 1969).

but they will experience severe problems of mobilization, communication, and coordination among both private and public organizations and at all levels of government.[3]

CONSTRUCTIVE RESPONSE TO PREDICTION

Given an earthquake prediction, what new measures can be taken to reduce the deaths, injuries, property losses, and disruptions just described? What more can we do if we are given advance warning of the approximate place, time, and magnitude of an impending quake than we could have done without the warning? The measures making up a complete program for utilizing an earthquake prediction can be grouped under five headings:

Authenticating and issuing predictions and warnings
Implementing a hazard-reduction program to minimize the loss of life and property and community disruption when the quake occurs
Readying emergency services to deal with the situation after the quake has occurred
Controlling and offsetting potentially counterproductive consequences of the prediction
Pre-prediction planning for each of the foregoing sets of tasks

PREDICTIONS AND WARNINGS

Detection of signs tending to indicate that a serious earthquake is in the offing immediately raises a series of questions about announcing the prediction and issuing warnings. When and how should information be made public? What kinds of reactions to the announcement are to be expected? What are the problems in making the prediction and warnings credible, and in motivating and enabling people to take life-preserving actions? These questions are the subject of Chapter 4. They are also discussed in connection with the political process, in Chapter 6, and they receive some consideration in connection with the problem of equity, in Chapter 7.

---

[3]For a discussion of misconceptions about human behavior and social responses to disasters see Charles E. Fritz, "Disaster," *Contemporary Social Problems,* Robert K. Merton and Robert A. Nisbet (ed.) (New York: Harcourt, Brace & World, Inc., 1961), pp. 651–694; and E. L. Quarantelli and Russell Dynes, "When Disaster Strikes: It Isn't Much Like What You've Heard and Read About," *Psychology Today,* 5 (February 1972), 66–70.

HAZARD REDUCTION

The opportunity to mount a carefully considered program of hazard reduction before the quake occurs is the unique and potentially most important contribution of earthquake prediction to saving lives and property and averting community disruption. The elements of such a program constitute the principal content of Chapter 9. However, we outline here some of the main possible kinds of hazard-reduction activity, as a basis for the discussions in all subsequent chapters of the report. Not all hazard-reduction measures will be applicable in all situations. Especially in our discussions of economic, legal, and political implications of earthquake prediction (Chapters 5, 6, and 8) we shall examine some of the obstacles to applying various hazard-reduction measures. But we assume that public officials charged with developing hazard-reduction programs for their own communities will wish to start with a list of possible steps, from which they can select those most promising in view of local conditions.

Evacuating Dangerous Localities and Vacating Vulnerable Structures

With our present understanding of future earthquake-prediction capabilities, we will be able to identify the location of the anticipated quake with considerable confidence. Accordingly, evacuation from selected areas will merit consideration in some cases. On the other hand, apart from the danger of landslides and tsunamis, the earth movements produced by a quake are generally not directly lethal to individuals in the affected area. Death and injury come principally from the collapse of buildings and other vulnerable structures and from fires ignited in or near them. Individuals at a safe distance from buildings and away from the course of flood waters occasioned by a collapsed dam can usually experience a quake in relative safety. Accordingly, general evacuation of a large area need seldom be considered. But selective evacuation of specific locations made vulnerable by the placement of dams, by the prospect of tsunamis, by the proximity of structures that are not resistant to seismic disturbance, and by the risk of fire and release of toxic materials may be desirable in some cases. Vacating unsafe buildings will merit careful study in each case.

Land-Use Planning

Land-use planning is a continuing responsibility of local governments. Several years of advance warning before a serious earthquake will provide the community with exceptional opportunities to employ their land-use management and control powers. Some relocation of lifelines away from the most vulnerable areas and some relocation of crucial public and private activities may be possible in many cases. The difficulties of using these powers indiscriminately and of making radical alterations in already established land-use plans will become evident as we discuss economic, legal, and political implications. Nevertheless, with long periods of advance warning, land-use management can often be a potent tool for reducing death and injury, property loss, and community disruption when a serious earthquake does occur.

Applying Structural Design and Maintenance Programs

Building codes and associated regulations are also among the standard tools at the disposal of local governments. In some cases a prediction may be the occasion for enacting new and more rigorous standards of protection; in other instances the application of existing standards can be accelerated and made stricter. The problem of dealing with existing structures that do not meet acceptable safety standards is more difficult, but communities will wish to explore carefully the legal resources and economic incentives at their disposal. Insofar as economic and legal considerations justify it, communities may wish to explore the desirability and practicability of demolishing unsafe structures before the quake. As the predicted time of the quake approaches, the issuance of permits for new construction may be suspended in some cases to lessen the danger from the collapse of unfinished structures.

Reducing Special Hazards to the Community

At the time of a prediction, leaders in the affected community will need to develop plans for reducing potential special risks. Such steps as lowering the water level behind dams; reassessing the safety features in facilities for the manufacture, transportation, and storage of toxic, chemically reactive, and radioactive materials; and dealing with local fire hazards may be considered.

Launching a Comprehensive Program of Public Information and Education

The novelty of earthquake prediction, the lack of public experience with destructive quakes because of their infrequency in any specific location, and the absence of publicly observable signs that a quake is imminent all contribute to the distinctive problems of devising a suitable public information program. Undoubtedly federal, state, and local governments and some private agencies will wish to consider how best to keep the public informed of the situation and of the advantages and disadvantages of various responses to the prediction.

READYING EMERGENCY SERVICES

Once a prediction is at hand, the second and third components come into play. The most readily understandable tasks are those of readying emergency services—for example, readying all rescue forces, including public and private agencies; identifying alternative transportation routes and communication lines; and assuring adequate and appropriately dispersed emergency equipment and supplies. We have not devoted a great deal of space to these tasks because the more forward-looking communities already have well-developed emergency-response plans that can be adapted to the new exigency of earthquake prediction. Careful planning in these respects should make important contributions toward saving lives and minimizing community disruption and, indirectly, toward reducing property loss and personal suffering.

DEALING WITH COUNTERPRODUCTIVE CONSEQUENCES OF PREDICTION

The prospect of a long period of advance warning and an extended time window for the anticipated occurrence combine to make possible certain responses to prediction that may weaken the community's economic base and impede effective community action. From a national perspective, these adjustments can be viewed as economically and socially desirable; from the perspective of the area or community affected, however, they would undoubtedly be viewed as negative consequences.

Without prior experience with earthquake prediction, we can only speculate about such counterproductive consequences. Perhaps there will be some outflow of capital from the area, some reluctance by lending agencies to grant mortgages for construction and purchase of homes and other buildings, and a refusal by insurance companies to issue certain kinds of insurance. Such consequences in turn may produce unemployment and reduce tax revenues to support the local government, in addition to undermining community morale and creating new occasions for political dissension. If such developments appear likely, affected communities will have to find ways to cope with them, as well as preparing for the actual earthquake. The potentially counterproductive responses are discussed in Chapters 5 through 9.

PRE-PREDICTION PLANNING

We mention pre-prediction planning because most of the activities we have outlined can be handled more effectively if plans have been worked out carefully before any earthquake prediction is made.

CONCLUSION

Our review of the sources of earthquake death and injury, property loss, and community disruption points to the failure of buildings and other forms of construction as the principal danger. Except for the evacuation of areas threatened by tsunamis and landslides, communities must act principally to protect people from the danger associated with vulnerable buildings and structures. Subsequent chapters of the report will deal with the problems of authenticating and issuing predictions and warnings, implementing a hazard-reduction program to minimize the loss of life and property and community disruption when the quake occurs, readying emergency services to deal with the situation after the quake has occurred, controlling and offsetting potentially counterproductive consequences of the prediction, and planning before any prediction for each of the foregoing sets of tasks.

SELECTED REFERENCES

Adams, David S. *Emergency Actions and Disaster Reactions: An Analysis of the Anchorage Public Works Department in the 1964 Alaska Earthquake.* Columbus, Ohio: Disaster Research Center, Monograph No. 5, 1969.

Anderson, William. *Disaster and Organizational Change: A Study of the Long-Term Consequences in Anchorage of the 1964 Alaska Earthquake.* Columbus, Ohio: Disaster Research Center, Monograph No. 6, 1969.

Committee on the Alaska Earthquake, National Research Council. *The Great Alaska Earthquake of 1964: Human Ecology.* Washington, D.C.: National Academy of Sciences, 1970.

Duke, C. M., and D. F. Moran. "Earthquakes and City Lifelines," *The San Fernando Earthquake of February 9, 1971, and Public Policy.* Special Subcommittee of the Joint Committee on Seismic Safety, California Legislature. Sacramento: California Legislature, 1972.

Dynes, Russell R., E. L. Quarantelli, and Gary Kreps. *A Perspective on Disaster Planning.* Columbus, Ohio: Disaster Research Center, Report Series No. 11, 1972.

Fritz, Charles E. "Disaster," *Contemporary Social Problems,* Robert K. Merton and Robert A. Nisbet (ed.). New York: Harcourt, Brace & World, Inc., 1961. pp. 651–694.

Iacopi, Robert. *Earthquake Country.* Menlo Park, California: Lane Books, 1964.

International Conference of Building Officials. *Uniform Building Code.* Whittier, California: International Conference of Building Officials, 1973.

Newmark, N. M., and E. Rosenblueth. *Fundamentals of Earthquake Engineering.* Englewood Cliffs, N.J.: Prentice-Hall, 1971.

Office of Emergency Preparedness, Executive Office of the President. *Disaster Preparedness,* Vol. III. Washington, D.C.: U.S. Government Printing Office, 1972.

Quarantelli, E. L., and Russell Dynes. "When Disaster Strikes: It Isn't Much Like What You've Heard and Read About," *Psychology Today,* 5 (February 1972), 66–70.

Richter, Charles F. *Elementary Seismology.* San Francisco: W. H. Freeman and Company, 1958.

Steinbrugge, Karl V. "Earthquake Damage and Structural Performance in the United States," *Earthquake Engineering,* R. L. Wiegel, (ed.). Englewood Cliffs, N.J.: Prentice-Hall, 1970.

White, Gilbert F., and J. Eugene Haas. *Assessment of Research on Natural Hazards.* Cambridge, Mass.: The MIT Press, 1975.

Yutzy, Daniel, William Anderson, and Russell Dynes. *Community Priorities in the Anchorage, Alaska, Earthquake, 1964.* Columbus, Ohio: Disaster Research Center, Monograph No. 4, 1969.

4 Issuing Predictions and Warnings

A crucial question for public policy is how to release earthquake predictions and issue warnings in such a way that the response will be constructive and not counterproductive. Because there have been no studies of how people and organizations respond to earthquake predictions and warnings, it is necessary to turn to other sources in seeking answers to this question. Three sources appear to be relevant: previous studies of responses to warning in disasters; analyses of long-term disaster-preparedness problems; and analyses of such slowly developing social problems as the energy and environmental crises. In the first part of this chapter each of these sources will be briefly examined for hints about expected responses to the release of earthquake predictions and warnings.

A *prediction* is a neutral statement that accumulated observations seem to signal more or less clearly the occurrence of an earthquake of a specified magnitude at a specified location and time. A *warning*, on the other hand, is a declaration that normal life routines should be altered for a time to deal with a danger impending or at hand. Predictions are based on science; they involve the detection, measurement, and evaluation of changes in the environment that could result in a danger of one sort or another. Warnings, on the other hand, are interpretations of predictions that take public policy into account.

EXPECTED RESPONSES TO EARTHQUAKE PREDICTIONS AND WARNINGS

STUDIES OF DISASTER WARNINGS

Warning provides a threatened population with information concerning the existence of danger and what can be done to prevent, avoid, or minimize it. As Williams points out, the warning involves the following steps:

1. Detection and measurement or estimation of changes in the environment which could result in a danger of one sort or another.
2. Collation and evaluation of the incoming information about environmental changes.
3. Decisions on who should be warned, about what danger, and in what way.
4. Transmission of warning message, or messages, to those whom it has been decided to warn.
5. Interpretation of the warning message by the recipients and action by the recipients.
6. Feedback of information about the interpretation and actions of recipients to the issuers of warning messages.
7. New warnings, if possible and desirable, corrected in terms of responses to the first warning messages.[1]

Many studies of responses to warning have been conducted in both peacetime and wartime disasters and and in false air raid alerts. These studies indicate that there are serious difficulties in achieving appropriate individual and organizational responses to warning, especially when people have had no recent experience with disaster or cannot actually perceive danger in their immediate surroundings. The common human tendency is to deny that danger is at hand unless events clearly indicate otherwise; and this usually means that the burden of proof is placed on the persons or agencies that issue the warning.

Difficulties in public warning often start with the persons or agencies responsible for detecting the danger and issuing the warnings. They are usually reluctant to issue a specific prediction or warning until they are reasonably certain that danger will actually materialize. Waiting for this degree of certainty has sometimes delayed the dissemination of the warning until it is too late. Warnings have sometimes been withheld or delayed because officials have held the stereotyped belief that people generally panic if warned. Extensive evidence from many disaster studies indicates that this belief is untrue.[2]

---

[1]Harry B. Williams, "Human Factors in Warning-and-Response Systems," *The Threat of Impending Disaster: Contributions to the Psychology of Stress,* George H. Grosser and others (ed.) (Cambridge: MIT Press, 1964), pp. 79–104.

[2]Charles E. Fritz, "Disaster," *Contemporary Social Problems,* Robert K. Merton and Robert A. Nisbet (ed.) (New York: Harcourt, Brace & World, Inc., 1961), pp. 651–694; and E. L. Quarantelli and Russell Dynes, "When Disaster Strikes: It Isn't Much Like What You've Heard and Read About," *Psychology Today,* 5 (February 1972), 66–70.

Even where the existence, nature, and time of the danger can be adequately forecast, it is difficult to secure public acceptance of warning messages. People tend to seize on any vagueness, ambiguity, or incompatibility in the warning message that enables them to interpret the situation optimistically. They search for more information that will confirm, deny, or clarify the warning message, and often they continue to interpret signs of danger as familiar, normal events until it is too late to take effective precautions and protective measures.[3]

Many of the difficulties in obtaining the desired response to warning stem from an oversimplified conception held by persons issuing warning information. They often conceive of warning as a direct, stimulus-response type of communication, in which the person issuing the warning gives the signal "danger" and people automatically respond as though danger were imminent. This view ignores the many social and personal influences that enter into people's interpretation of danger and their response to it. In deciding whether danger exists, people use their past experience, their present direct perceptions of the physical environment, their perceptions of how others are responding, and their comparison of their own information and perceptions with those of people who are significant to them in their daily lives. In deciding how to respond to a danger signal, people also take into account the nature and strength of the threat, the time available before the predicted disaster strikes, the effectiveness of available countermeasures, and the cost (in time, effort, personal sacrifice, or money). If they are not fully persuaded that the threat is real, however, they may give no further thought to other elements in the situation.[4]

An effective disaster-warning system requires a realistic recognition of these social and personal responses to information about danger. As noted in the foregoing definition of warning, the agency issuing the warning must not only transmit messages about the existence of danger but also supply people with information about what can be done to avoid or reduce the danger. To ensure that people are really acting in pursuit of their own safety, the warning agency must also have the capacity to ascertain that people are correctly interpreting and acting upon the warning information.[5]

These findings and guidelines from previous disaster-warning studies have general relevance to the earthquake prediction, warning, and response process. We would not expect most people to respond to the

[3] Fritz, *op. cit.*
[4] Paul Slovic, Howard Kunreuther, Gilbert F. White, "Decision Processes, Rationality, and Adjustment to Natural Hazards," *Natural Hazards: Local, National, and Global,* Gilbert F. White (ed.) (New York: Oxford Press, 1974), pp. 187–205.
[5] Fritz, *op. cit.*; Williams, *op. cit.*

release of earthquake predictions and the issuance of earthquake warnings with panic, hysteria, or other nonrational or uncontrolled forms of behavior. On the contrary, a much more likely response derives from the so-called "normalcy bias"[6]—i.e., the tendency for people to accept most readily any information that enables them to disbelieve the prediction, minimize the danger, and view the situation optimistically. There is likely to be sufficient ambiguity in earthquake predictions and warnings, especially the ones released during the next few years, to allow people to convince themselves either that no real danger exists or that the danger is so far in the future that they can defer taking any type of precautionary or protective action. This will be reinforced by the absence of the kinds of readily observable changes in the physical environment that confirm the presence of danger in floods, hurricanes, and tornadoes.

The normalcy bias will also be reinforced by the long lead times from the time of initial warning until the actual occurrence of an earthquake. Past disaster studies suggest that the more remote in time the anticipated impact, the less likely people are to take adaptive actions.[7] Responsible authorities will have a difficult task during the period following earthquake predictions and warnings to keep the threatened population from becoming complacent.

The national attention focused on the designated area may lead to the so-called "convergence" of people and messages toward the threatened area or toward centers of information and communication in or near the area.[8] Although convergence is normally associated with the mass movement of people, messages, and supplies toward an area already hit by disaster, it is conceivable that some forms of convergence may result solely from the release of earthquake predictions and warnings. For example, the agencies releasing earthquake predictions and warnings may find themselves deluged by visiting scientists, government officials, mass media representatives, and businessmen who seek additional information about the predicted earthquake. Numerous telephone, telegraph, and letter queries from the general public may also be directed to such agencies and to the mass information media. Convergence may also take the form of curious outsiders touring the area of predicted danger. As the

[6]Benjamin F. McLuckie, *The Warning System: A Social Science Perspective,* National Oceanic and Atmospheric Administration, United States Department of Commerce (Washington, D.C.: U.S. Government Printing Office, 1973), p. 22.
[7]Dennis Mileti and Sigmund Krane, "Countdown to the Unlikely" (Paper presented at the annual meeting of the American Sociological Association, New York City, August 1973).
[8]Charles E. Fritz and J. H. Mathewson, *Convergence Behavior in Disasters: A Problem in Social Control* (Washington, D.C.: National Academy of Sciences–National Research Council, Publication 476, 1957).

time of the predicted quake approaches, this may even include some thrill seekers who wish to be present to observe and experience the quake itself. Such convergence responses may temporarily overload the capacities of existing transportation and communication networks and severely tax the work capabilities of various agencies involved in formulating, disseminating, and responding to predictions and warnings.

As in the case of other disaster predictions and warnings, public officials responsible for issuing earthquake warnings are likely to delay until they are reasonably satisfied that the danger will actually develop. Officials will be concerned about what false alarms will do to their credibility and future effectiveness; they may also be concerned with the legal problems associated with erroneous predictions. The lack of precision in early earthquake predictions—in terms of time, location, and magnitude of the projected events—will subject public officials to great pressures and perhaps also make them hesitant to try to convince the population at risk that the predictions are valid. These and related considerations have led Haas to suggest that "Public officials in the areas to which the earthquake forecast applies will try to avoid taking a position publicly on the probable validity of the forecast. To the extent that this is impossible, their comments and actions will tend to undermine the credibility of the forecast."[9]

Previous disaster research on warnings also suggests that there will be differences in people's responses to earthquake predictions and warnings, depending on such characteristics as their previous disaster experience and their social and cultural characteristics. Most research findings suggest that it is easier to obtain a desirable response to disaster warnings from groups that have had recent disaster experience.[10] Groups residing in areas exposed to recurrent disaster threats tend to build cultural defenses against them, including organized ways of responding to warnings. In some of these areas, referred to as "disaster cultures" in the research literature,[11] public officials and citizens alike show a high degree of sensitivity to the threat of disaster. The implication for earthquake

[9]J. Eugene Haas, "Forecasting the Consequences of Earthquake Forecasting," *Social Science Perspectives on the Coming San Francisco Earthquake: Economic Impact, Prediction, and Reconstruction,* Natural Hazard Research Working Paper No. 25 (Boulder, Colorado: University of Colorado Institute of Behavioral Science, 1974), p. 50.

[10]William A. Anderson, "Tsunami Warning in Crescent City, California, and Hilo, Hawaii," *The Great Alaska Earthquake of 1964: Human Ecology,* Committee on the Alaska Earthquake, National Research Council (Washington, D.C.: National Academy of Sciences, 1970), pp. 116–124.

[11]Harry E. Moore, . . . *and the Winds Blew* (Austin: Hogg Foundation for Mental Health, University of Texas Press, 1964), pp. 195–213; and Russell R. Dynes, *Organized Behavior in Disaster* (Lexington, Mass.: D. C. Heath, 1970), p. 92.

predictions is that we might expect the responses to warning of communities in California, with a well-known history of considerable seismic activity, to be quite different from the responses of communities in Missouri, which is subject to earthquake risk but has had much less seismic activity. If an earthquake-disaster culture has developed in California communities, the threatened populations there would be more likely to assign credibility to earthquake predictions and thus respond appropriately than would threatened populations in communities with no recent earthquake experience. Moreover, Los Angeles and many other California communities would not have to start from scratch in responding to an earthquake warning because they already have programs geared to reducing the earthquake hazard, such as construction regulations to make buildings and other structures earthquake-resistant.

It should be emphasized, however, that past experiences with a hazard do not invariably produce the needed protective actions by the threatened population. For example, some communities subject to periodic flooding gear their responses to the largest flood that can be reasonably expected within an extended time period, such as a "hundred-year flood." They are then unprepared for the unexpected flood of greater magnitude. Many California communities have been subjected to only minor earthquakes for the past several decades, and many of their inhabitants may take an earthquake warning lightly because of their past experiences with minor, nondestructive quakes.

On the basis of existing disaster studies, we expect the greatest difficulty in securing desirable responses to earthquake predictions and warnings from people outside the mainstream of society.[12] This group includes elderly people, the handicapped, those of lower socioeconomic status, and members of various ethnic and minority groups. People in these groups are especially likely not to receive, understand, or believe earthquake warnings. Foreign-speaking ethnic groups may not understand earthquake-warning messages given in English. Because of past grievances and hostilities, many members of minority groups may have difficulty believing the disseminators of earthquake warnings. Such grievances and hostilities may undermine or diminish the credibility of the official sources issuing the predictions and warnings and thereby increase the possibility that large numbers of the population at risk will not take appropriate precautionary and protective actions.

These findings from previous disaster-warning research are useful in identifying many of the problems that are likely to characterize earth-

---

[12]Mileti and Krane, *op. cit.*

quake predictions and warnings, but their relevance is limited because the conditions in which they were derived are not directly analogous to those that will pertain in earthquake prediction. It is important to note these differences:

1. The disaster events previously studied (e.g., floods, hurricanes, tornadoes, explosions) have had much shorter warning times than those projected for earthquake predictions. In the former case, the elapsed time between prediction and occurrence of the disaster consists of minutes, hours, days (e.g., hurricanes) or, at most, weeks (some river floods). In the case of potentially destructive earthquakes, much longer periods of advance warning are anticipated.

2. Unlike floods, hurricanes, and tornadoes, earthquakes are preceded by no clearly detectable external signs by which the public can confirm through their own senses that an earthquake will shortly occur, could have occurred, or still may occur. This will make earthquakes unique among predicted disasters in the extent to which public response will depend exclusively on the faith people are willing to place in scientific prediction.

3. Damaging earthquakes of 6.0 magnitude or higher occur so infrequently in any specific locality in the United States that every prediction of such a quake is likely to be the first such experience in the lifetimes of most of the inhabitants of the affected area and of most of the personnel charged with preparing for the event. Hence, the accumulation of experience by personnel in a local area cannot provide the basis for constructive action in response to warnings of an impending earthquake (as they might in areas frequently affected by floods, hurricanes, and other recurrent natural disasters).

4. False alarms in earthquake predictions and warnings are likely to be more costly and disruptive— at least in the short run—because the longer lead times permit more extensive and costly adjustments and preparedness measures than are possible in connection with other disasters (hurricanes, floods, tornadoes) with comparatively brief warning periods. Viewed in the long run, many of the immediate costs may contribute to the community's defense against *any* earthquake.

These qualitatively different characteristics of earthquake prediction indicate the need to search elsewhere for analogous conditions or, at least, for types of human experience that offer a closer fit. In the following two sections, we shall look for additional insights into likely responses to earthquake predictions and warnings by examining long-term disaster-preparedness problems and such slowly developing social problems as the energy crisis.

LONG-TERM DISASTER-PREPAREDNESS PROBLEMS

How do communities and societies respond to calls for long-term disaster-preparedness planning? Studies show clearly that the most highly organized preparation exists in communities and societies that have repeatedly and recently experienced the same kind of disaster. Thus in coal-mining communities, where there is an ever-present danger of disaster, there is usually a well-developed system of rescue and relief operations. Similarly, many areas frequently affected by floods and hurricanes have developed institutional mechanisms of warning and relief, and families have worked out informal precautionary, protective, and ameliorative methods of coping with the destructive and disruptive effects of such disasters.[13]

In general, however, highly organized and effective long-term preparations for disaster are exceptional; most communities and societies have not prepared adequate technological, social, and psychological defenses against the hazards to which they are vulnerable. Surveys concerning the status of both peacetime and wartime disaster preparations have consistently shown that only a small percentage of the population will voluntarily undertake preparations to cope with uncertain future disasters. And the adequacy of community preparedness plans and programs throughout the United States is highly variable—ranging from well organized and effective to nonexistent. For example, both Crescent City, California, and Hilo, Hawaii, have been subjected to tsunamis. In Hilo, following a major tsunami disaster in 1960, steps were taken to combat this hazard, including allocation of increased resources to emergency organizations, identification of high-risk areas, and development of an evacuation plan. In contrast, little long-term emergency planning has been undertaken in Crescent City, despite the fact that it, too, experienced a tsunami disaster that took lives and destroyed property.[14]

With particular reference to earthquakes, there has been a general failure to adopt such long-term hazard-reduction programs as land-use planning and building regulations designed to protect against seismic disturbance. As noted in Chapter 3, this is generally true for all states in the nation except California and Alaska, but even in the high-seismic-risk areas of those states many communities have failed either to adopt

[13]Fritz, *op. cit.*
[14]Anderson, *op. cit.*

or to enforce adequate programs of this type. Various constraints and resistances operate against such programs. Building codes, for example, mean added costs for enforcement for owners and the government. Condemnation of old buildings breaks up existing neighborhoods, creates relocation problems, and can enhance conflict among special-interest groups.[15] It is difficult to secure agreement and cooperation among so many different persons and groups: owners, engineers, architects, builders, lending institutions, insurance companies, and government officials.

All of this indicates that it is extremely difficult to achieve an adequate state of preparation under ordinary conditions, especially when there has been no recent previous experience with disaster and the threat seems highly indefinite or uncertain. Groups advocating disaster preparedness must compete with others who want limited national or local resources used for more immediate, imperative, or well-defined social needs. This competition is inherently unequal; long-range disaster-preparedness programs and plans, at all levels of government and at the family level, are often sacrificed for other more pressing social and personal concerns.[16] There is a real danger that the usual preoccupation with immediate and pressing social and personal concerns will prevent the adoption and implementation of those long-term preparedness plans and programs that will be most effective in saving lives, reducing property losses, and minimizing social disruption.

SLOWLY DEVELOPING SOCIAL PROBLEMS (THE ENERGY CRISIS)

The initial efforts to secure constructive responses to earthquake predictions and warnings may be analogous to efforts to mobilize the government and people to deal with such critical national social problems as environmental pollution and the energy shortage. For present purposes, we will concentrate attention on the possible similarities between the so-called energy crisis and efforts to develop and sustain a coherent preparedness program in response to earthquake predictions and warnings.

The current problems arising from the domestic shortage of oil and natural gas have been developing slowly but inexorably over many years. As early as 1956, the geologist M. King Hubbert predicted the present U.S. shortage of oil and gas resources. At that time, he stated that oil production would peak in 10–15 years and then begin to decline. The petroleum industry first reacted to Hubbert's predictions with dismay

[15]Gilbert F. White and J. Eugene Haas, *Assessment of Research on Natural Hazards* (Cambridge, Mass.: The MIT Press, 1975).
[16]Fritz, *op. cit.*

and disbelief and then attempted to disprove his statements.[17] Subsequently, various other interest groups entered into the public debate by forecasting damaging consequences to the United States if it did not curb its excessive use of energy resources, increase domestic production of the fossil fuels, or develop alternative sources of energy supply.

Despite these forecasts and the developing debate on energy problems, however, the American public showed no basic awareness of, or concern for, the growing energy shortage. It took an Arab oil boycott, starting in October, 1973, to draw the country's attention to our declining capacity to meet our growing energy needs and to make the phrase "energy crisis" meaningful.

The public response to the government's call for energy conservation during the oil boycott was generally favorable. Speed limits on the highways were lowered, many industries and businesses voluntarily cut back on their use of energy, and families and individuals attempted to do their part by forming car pools, lowering the temperature in their houses, and purchasing smaller, energy-efficient autos. However, the resulting public awareness and the impetus to develop basic societal changes in solving the nation's long-term energy problems were relatively short-lived. Within a year's time, numerous observers reported that the government had failed to exert adequate leadership in developing a coherent program to solve the country's long-term energy problems. At one point, the President, to the dismay of many, even publicly declared that the energy crisis was over. A year later, automobile manufacturers had grudgingly made limited shifts in production quotas toward smaller cars, and automobile drivers remained ambivalent about reduced speed limits. In a news program aired on July 28, 1974, entitled "Whatever Happened to the Energy Crisis?" CBS had asked, "How are you going to get action before the day of reckoning?" The same question is relevant for earthquake predictions and warnings.

There has been little or no systematic social science research on the U.S. energy crisis, so the evidence in this area is admittedly less certain than in the two previous subject areas that we have drawn on for assessing expected future responses to earthquake predictions and warnings. It appears, however, that the energy crisis comprises a somewhat more valid analogy—at least for some of the expected responses—than the

---

[17]Robert Gillette, "Oil and Gas Resources: Academy Calls USGS Math Misleading," *Science*, 18 (February 28, 1975), 723–727. This article is based on *Mineral Resources and the Environment* by the Committee on Mineral Resources and the Environment, Commission on Natural Resources, National Research Council (Washington, D.C.: National Academy of Sciences, 1975).

other two bodies of evidence, so it may be useful to draw some inferences from it.

The energy crisis raises serious questions about the length of time required to draw the necessary attention to the earthquake hazard so that responses to warnings will be adequate. It also raises doubts about sustaining that awareness once it is developed. Predictions covering long time spans are usually marked by considerable uncertainty and are greeted with skepticism in many segments of society.

A lack of consensus on the validity and value of earthquake prediction may spawn opposing interest groups and countermovements. The merits and credibility of such predictions will be debated in scientific circles and by various interest groups, utilizing the mass media of communication. The opposition of some scientists and engineers to the development of an operational earthquake-prediction system is already beginning to surface. This opposition is based on a variety of doubts and fears: scientific skepticism about the current theoretical underpinnings for earthquake prediction; fears that increased emphasis on prediction will detract from or undermine continuing efforts to achieve improved hazard reduction in earthquake-prone areas; fears that inaccurate predictions will undermine scientific credibility; and fears that predictions may produce "mass panic" among the affected populace. A popular theme currently being espoused among some scientists and science popularizers is that "prediction might be more devastating than the event itself."[18]

With the advent of specific, credible predictions, various businesses and other groups whose economic, social, and political interests are adversely affected by a prediction may publicly oppose the acceptance of the predictions and urge that no action be taken on the warning (see Chapters 5, 6, and 8). Especially during the early developmental phase of earthquake-prediction technology, they are likely to attack the credibility of the predictions and warnings by pointing to the uncertainties in the state of the art, to alternative explanations for the precursory signs used as evidence by the persons and agencies issuing the predictions and warnings, to inaccuracies in previous predictions, to earlier false alarms, and so on. Large-scale businesses will undoubtedly hire their own seismologists to evaluate the evidence, and, in some cases, such seismologists may be utilized to refute the prediction or to cast doubt on its validity and reliability. The resulting differences of judgment among presumably equally qualified experts are likely to cause the public officials to resist taking positive action on the prediction.

[18]Garrett Hardin, "Earthquakes: Prediction More Devastating Than Events," *Stalking the Wild Taboo* (Los Altos, California: William Kaufmann, Inc., 1973), pp. 123–134. Also see news item in *Geotimes,* April 1974, p. 28.

SUMMARY

This examination of previous disaster warning studies, of long-term disaster-preparedness problems, and of the energy crisis leads us to conclude that securing adequate, constructive responses to earthquake warnings will not be an easy task. Experience with other disasters suggests that warnings may be widely discounted and ignored and that inaction rather than panic flight will be the most common response among the general public. Especially in case of long-term predictions, the remoteness of the threat will impart a sense of unreality. The absence of external signs through which people can confirm the threat with their own senses creates a special problem of credibility.

Previous experience with efforts to achieve an adequate state of disaster preparedness in the predisaster phase also shows that, in the absence of a recent experience with a devastating earthquake, long-range hazard-reduction and emergency-preparedness plans and programs will be very difficult to establish and maintain.

Our brief examination of the U.S. energy crisis tends to reinforce these conclusions. It will be difficult to achieve consensus on the validity of predictions and what should be done in response to them, especially during the early phases in the development of an operational predictive system.

All this does not mean that there is no hope of achieving adequate, constructive responses to earthquake predictions and warnings. It does mean that these resistances and constraints must be squarely confronted by the relevant federal, state, and local officials in the development of earthquake-prediction and warning-response systems. Officials must take major responsibility for planning and implementing a coherent, continuing program of hazard reduction and disaster preparedness. To the extent that this program requires public participation, the leadership must specify the realistic nature of future danger, the means for dealing effectively with the danger, and the concrete steps needed to secure the required state of preparation prior to the quake's impact. Means for facilitating public compliance with the requirements of the plan must also be incorporated in the program of preparation.

The development of this coherent earthquake prediction and warning system will require cooperation among scientists, public officials, and the communication media to provide understandable and unsensational interpretations of reported predictions. A continuing informational program is needed to ensure that public officials and citizens learn directly from scientists the nature of their thinking about earthquake mechanisms and prediction. Public officials, the media, and the general public will

Issuing Predictions and Warnings 59

require the advice of a disinterested group of scientists in distinguishing valid from doubtful predictions. Cooperation of the communication media will be important in helping people to visualize the laboratories, the seismographic networks, and the panoply of instruments and devices through which predictions are developed. Outlining concrete response plans should help to add a sense of reality to the warnings as well as to forestall some disorganized and disruptive responses. The development of constructive ways in which citizens and groups can participate actively in the preparedness program should also help to bolster public credence. Emergency plans should provide for activation of citizen involvement directly upon issuance of a warning, with intensified and broadened involvement as the predicted time approaches.

Many of the problems that may be expected on the basis of past experience will, of course, tend to diminish if a successful record of accurate predictions of major damaging earthquakes is established. This will be especially true if it can be shown that the hazard-reduction and emergency-preparedness measures taken on the basis of predictions and warnings were highly effective in saving lives, preserving property, and minimizing social disruption.

STRATEGIES FOR ISSUING WARNINGS

Formulating effective earthquake-warning strategies begins with identifying focal points for action in the public interest: action to promote an understanding of the prediction and its implications; preparedness measures that achieve a reasonable balance between the need to preserve lives and the desire to protect property; and the need to minimize disruption to both the economy and the way of life in communities affected by the prediction.

Earthquakes of magnitude 5 and less do not constitute sufficient threats to life and the economy to justify all-out preparedness measures. Strategy-building efforts must be focused on predictions of earthquakes in the magnitude range of 6 and above. Such potentially destructive quakes may sometimes be predicted with a lead time of a decade or more, but the time window within which they are to occur may be specified only within months or a year or more, at least initially. Early planning for these events must therefore focus on such measures as land-use management, building codes, structural upgrading, condemnation of unsafe structures, and educational programs to prepare the public gradually for an event many years away.

Before specific strategies can be devised, it is necessary to decide on the general role to be played by federal, state, and local governments and private agencies with regard to predictions, verification of predictions, preparedness planning, and public warnings. Most earthquake predictions will originate with individual scientists or the private institutions they represent. Information concerning these predictions first reaches the public directly through the media from a release by the scientist or his sponsors. What responsibility, if any, should reside with federal, state, and local governments for explicit follow-up action when such predictions are issued? Are there advantages in having nationwide uniform procedures for evaluating predictions and for issuing public warnings, or should leaders in each earthquake-prone area be encouraged to tailor their own earthquake-warning preparedness measures to local needs? Finally, if government should play an active or even authoritative role in connection with earthquake predictions and warnings, how should it be involved?

THE GENERATION AND RELEASE OF AN EARTHQUAKE PREDICTION

Research on earthquakes in the United States is mostly funded by the federal government. The research takes place within federal agencies, universities, and private research institutions. Scientists differ greatly in their dispositions toward early release of predictions. The competition for research funds, the importance for the scientific career of winning credit for being first with a significant discovery, and the public-relations benefit to the institution all foster early release. On the other hand, the damage to a scientific reputation from an ill-considered announcement, awareness of the uncertainty of public response to a prediction, and a fear of being harassed by the press, officials, cranks, and the general public will cause some scientists to withhold their announcements. The principal constraint on both premature or scientifically unwarranted release and undue delay or suppression is peer pressure.

In the case of the relatively short-fused warnings of hurricanes and tornadoes, a system has evolved through the years in which, by mutual consent, the private sector and all research interests recognize a single official source of public warnings upon which protective actions are based. In this case the source is in the federal government. Dissenting opinions or minority reports are rarely aired in the public media at the time of the event. In part, this "mutual consent" is given incentive by a law[19] holding the broadcaster or telecaster responsible for airing "false weather reports." There is no precedent that we know of in which puni-

[19] 18 U.S. Code, Sec. 2074, "False Weather Reports."

tive action has been taken under this law, and it is questionable whether a conflicting report would be construed as a "false report" in a court of law. Nevertheless, in severe-weather warnings the system works effectively.

When we recognize current limitations in the extent of understanding and agreement among seismologists and in the adequacy of instrumentation and baseline data, we cannot justify restricting the issuance of earthquake predictions to a single source, public or private. Because of the great public interest certain to be aroused by indications of an impending quake, it is doubtful that information leaks could be prevented by any means. Furthermore, efforts to prevent public release of predictions would inevitably stifle exchange of information among scientists. Stifling scientific exchange would retard progress in testing competing theories and generating new insights about earthquake prediction. Thus an important consequence of trying to establish a single agency for the release of predictions at the present time would be to postpone the day when scientists can agree confidently on the criteria for a valid prediction.

Stimulation of peer pressure is probably one of the more constructive ways in which the federal government can help to curb irresponsible issuance or unwarranted suppression of predictions. Governmental sponsorship and encouragement of constructive scientific review and debate and revision of predictive information upon which preparedness actions must be based should contribute to this end. The U.S. Geological Survey, together with other scientific organizations, can work in this way.

MACHINERY FOR PRESENTING CREDIBLE EARTHQUAKE WARNINGS TO THE PUBLIC

The earthquake prediction and warning process may be viewed as comprising four basic functions:

Developing and releasing the prediction
Evaluating the technical merit of the prediction
Determining appropriate response to the prediction
Actually disseminating the warning

We have suggested that no official machinery is needed for the first of these functions. Predictions will flow freely from a variety of scientific sources, both within and outside the federal government, as a result of the scientific freedom enjoyed in this country.

Evaluating the Technical Merit of the Prediction

The second function will depend partially upon the peer pressure that evolves from scientific forums for reviewing research results. Professional societies hold frequent technical conferences to report research and to subject it to evaluation and constructive criticism. These meetings generate considerable peer pressure against unsound scientific work and irresponsible publication. Where the public interest and welfare are explicitly involved, as in the case of earthquake predictions, the federal government should assume some role in stimulating and augmenting this peer pressure. This could be accomplished by organizing special symposia or workshops to examine and evaluate the evidence upon which predictions of important earthquakes are based and by publishing and widely disseminating the arguments and conclusions reached in the symposia. These symposia and workshops, perhaps funded by the federal government, could be organized through the established professional societies concerned with seismology. Another, more explicit, government role in connection with the task of evaluation could be to establish a publication medium whose primary function would be to update the predictions of earthquakes whenever there are any outstanding in areas of concern to the United States, and to present the results of new research and analyses that bear upon these predictions.

For the public official who must decide when to issue a warning and what kind of earthquake preparedness to initiate, it will not suffice that scientists are constantly evaluating each other's work. The official requires some recognized body of scientists to whom he can turn for a prompt, balanced, and unassailable evaluation of any prediction of a potentially destructive quake. The body must include scientists in both the public and private sectors, transcending the interests and approaches of any single agency or school of thought. The Governor of California has already established a panel on a standby basis. But few states have the resources in scientific personnel needed for such panels, and greatest credibility will be accorded a nationally based group, relatively detached from local and regional political scenes. Accordingly, a major function of the federal government should be to establish such a panel now. Steps should be taken promptly to devise a mode of operation that will ensure its effectiveness when the first prediction of a potentially destructive earthquake is issued.

Determining Appropriate Response

The effectiveness of programs to reduce exposure to natural hazards and lessen their impact depends largely on the initiative and intelligent involvement of government at the state and local levels. Furthermore, the state governor is traditionally and legally the one who calls for federal assistance in case of disaster and distributes much of the aid to affected communities. State and local initiative in performing this third function of determining the appropriate response to prediction allows taxpayers in the affected areas to establish priorities regarding expensive or disruptive earthquake-preparedness measures according to local rather than outside evaluation of their needs.

However, there is again an important role for the federal government to play. The federal government is in a more favorable position than state or local governments to provide technical advisory services in the face of local and regional political crosscurrents. Federal agencies are better equipped to accumulate experience with earthquakes and earthquake predictions under diverse sets of circumstances. On many grounds it appears in the national interest to devise a program for dealing uniformly with earthquake predictions wherever they occur—Tennessee, Massachusetts, South Carolina, Alaska, the Mountain States, or the West Coast. Such a program is unlikely to develop just from the example of one enlightened state government, such as that of California, or through such a national agency as the Council of State Governments. The federal government should assume the initiative in planning appropriate responses for suitably authenticated predictions. State and local leaders will retain the responsibility for initiating action when a prediction is made and for adapting standards to the local situation. But in preparation for the predictions, the federal government must serve as the focal point for formulating standards and guidelines for earthquake-preparatory measures, for developing seismological systems needed for achieving predictions, and for funding and stimulating earthquake-prediction research.

Disseminating Warnings

Formal issuance of a warning will often be a momentous step for the public official. Issuing the warning shifts the center of attention and responsibility from the scientists to the official. We discuss the impact of this responsibility more fully in Chapter 8, dealing with political implications of earthquake prediction. The most important immediate concern is that the prompt issuance of an earthquake warning, including assessment of risk, information concerning community plans, and advice for individual action, not be hindered by uncertainty concerning responsibility. Hence it is important that the federal government initiate discussion with representatives of governors in potentially affected states to establish responsibilities and procedures for the issuance of warnings. The decision may be to decentralize the warning process, particularly in the immediate future while predictive capability is restricted to a few states. In the more distant future the move may be toward a more centralized warning process. For the present, however, it is essential that questions of responsibility be resolved before the first serious earthquake is predicted.

Regardless of any decision to decentralize responsibility for warnings, the use of common terminologies, similar programs of public education, and fairly standard formats for communicating warnings and action advice to the public should be encouraged for use by all states. Selection of the terminology most suited to the circumstances of earthquake prediction will require further study. But there is considerable merit in employing terminology similar to that used for hurricanes, tornadoes, floods, and tsunamis. The following list is offered merely as an example of how the standard warning terminology might be adapted for earthquakes:

The Annual Outlook identifies explicit areas that are most vulnerable to earthquake activity, with an assessment of trends and lead time for action in cases in which premonitory signs have been noted.

An Earthquake Advisory is issued for a specific geographical area when significant premonitory signs have been identified for the first time. The *Advisory* specifies the probable location of the anticipated quake. It also indicates a time period expected to elapse before earthquake activity might begin. When possible, the expected magnitude should be reported. *Advisories* should be numbered and issued at regular intervals after the initial announcement.

An Earthquake Bulletin is an urgent action advice reserved for those rare occasions in which there is good evidence that significant earthquake activity is imminent—a few days to as much as 2 weeks—and that *extraordinary measures* should probably be initiated to minimize possible loss of life and property.

An Earthquake Watch might be used, in the same manner as the hurricane *Watch* and the tornado *Watch,* for areas that have been receiving regular *Advisories,* when there is compelling evidence that an earthquake of significant proportions can be expected within several months. The

Watch might precede the beginning of *Bulletin* issuance, but would apply to the same geographic area subsequently addressed in a *Bulletin*.

Whether or not present skills in earthquake prediction can be molded into a program acceptable to the public and useful in reducing loss of life and property will depend in part upon: (a) the development of an effective means of authenticating earthquake predictions and of defining and communicating the urgency of initiating preparedness measures to planning officials who must implement these measures; and (b) the development of effective procedures and terminologies for communicating information to the public, for implementing preparedness measures, and for explicitly warning the public. If a national program to serve this purpose is to be developed and is to grow with future advances in earthquake-prediction skills, there must be a carefully orchestrated effort by both federal and state governments that makes effective use of the unique resources and competencies inherent at the federal, state, and local levels of government.

SELECTED REFERENCES

Anderson, William A. "Tsunami Warning in Crescent City, California, and Hilo, Hawaii," *The Great Alaska Earthquake of 1964: Human Ecology,* Committee on the Alaska Earthquake, National Research Council. Washington, D.C.: National Academy of Sciences, 1970.

Dynes, Russell R. *Organized Behavior in Disaster.* Lexington, Mass.: D. C. Heath & Co., 1970.

Fritz, Charles E. "Disaster," *Contemporary Social Problems,* Robert K. Merton and Robert A. Nisbet (ed.). New York: Harcourt, Brace & World, Inc., 1961. pp. 651–694.

Fritz, Charles E. "Disasters," *International Encyclopedia of the Social Sciences.* New York: The MacMillan Company and The Free Press, 1968. pp. 202–207.

Haas, J. Eugene. "Forecasting the Consequences of Earthquake Forecasting," *Social Science Perspectives on the Coming San Francisco Earthquake: Economic Impact, Prediction, and Reconstruction,* Natural Hazard Research Working Paper No. 25. Boulder, Colorado: University of Colorado Institute of Behavioral Science, 1974.

Mack, Raymond W., and George W. Baker. *The Occasion Instant: The Structure of Social Responses to Unanticipated Air Raid Warnings,* Washington, D.C.: National Academy of Sciences–National Research Council Publication No. 945, 1961.

McLuckie, Benjamin F. *The Warning System: A Social Science Perspective.* National Oceanic and Atmospheric Administration, United States Department of Commerce. Washington, D.C.: U.S. Government Printing Office, March 1973.

McLuckie, Benjamin F. *Warning—A Call to Action.* National Oceanic and Atmospheric Administration, United States Department of Commerce. Washington, D.C.: U.S. Government Printing Office, March 1974.

Mileti, Dennis S., and Sigmund Krane. "Countdown: Response to the Unlikely." Paper presented at the annual meeting of the American Sociological Association, New York City, August 1973.

Quarantelli, E. L., and Russell R. Dynes. "When Disaster Strikes: It Isn't Much Like What You've Heard and Read About," *Psychology Today,* 5 (February 1972), 66–70.

Williams, Harry B. "Human Factors in Warning-and-Response Systems," *The Threat of Impending Disaster: Contributions to the Psychology of Stress,* George H. Grosser and others (ed.). Cambridge: MIT Press, 1964. pp. 79–104.

5 Economic Implications of Earthquake Prediction

This chapter explores two major sets of questions concerning the economic implications of earthquake prediction. First, what will be the economic reactions of businesses, households, and public agencies to the prediction itself? It is important in selecting preprediction and postprediction measures to understand how the economic system might respond to the new information. Will there be large-scale economic disruption because of the prediction? How will land markets and financial markets react? How will economic decision makers process the information? Assumptions about the economic reactions to the prediction will influence the kinds of overall adjustment mechanisms to be pursued. By the same token, policies for adjustment will clearly condition the economic response to the prediction.

A second set of questions deals with the benefits and costs of various kinds of hazard-reduction measures. For example, which is more economical from a social point of view—land-use zoning, the construction of earthquake-resistant structures, or the extension of insurance? The optimal mix of hazard-reduction measures is a function of the perceived probabilities that a quake will occur, but a prediction will change these subjective probabilities. What kinds of adjustments should be undertaken in the period following the issuance of a prediction? Concern has often been expressed that insufficient steps have been taken to reduce the earthquake hazard and to provide "acceptable" levels of risk, yet very little economic analysis has been undertaken to determine what might be desirable kinds and levels of adjustments under various assumptions about probabilities of risk. What adjustments are suitable for the public sector? What kinds of investments in hazard reduction should be undertaken in the private sector?

Mitigation of earthquake loss involves balancing the costs of adjustment taken prior to the event with the residual damage and recovery costs following the event. Properly handled, the ability to predict quakes with greater certainty can lead to rational actions aimed at minimizing the sum of the adjustment costs plus residual damage costs. Costs can never be eliminated, of course; they can only be minimized. Most measures involving predisaster adjustment involve trading resources between time periods and reduction of current production and consumption for the possibility of greater production and consumption following a quake. Some adverse economic effects are unavoidable, and shifting them in time is the rational way of attempting to minimize net social losses.

ECONOMIC REACTIONS TO AN EARTHQUAKE PREDICTION

In this section we will make a series of conjectures about plausible economic reactions to a credible earthquake prediction for a major urban area in the United States. It is assumed that the lead time is 5 to 10 years.

There are two principal reasons why this section must be largely conjectural: (a) We are considering a first-event case. After several predictions have been made and subsequent quakes are experienced, we will have more knowledge of how economic decision makers process information about earthquake predictions. Normative models for decision making under conditions of uncertainty do exist. However, empirical models for predicting the behavior of public agencies, private businesses, and households regarding low-probability events are not equally available. (b) We cannot begin to understand the dynamic interactions of the components of the regional economy without the aid of fairly sophisticated regional economic models.

DECISIONS FOR PROBABILISTIC EVENTS

Efficient economic adjustment to earthquake predictions requires understanding of the probabilistic character of the event itself, a probabilistic assessment of the correctness of the prediction and a probabilistic assessment of the payoffs of various adjustment mechanisms. At present our knowledge of these various probabilities is very limited. Normative models for decision making under conditions of uncertainty cannot be very helpful until a better basis for assessing the various probabilities is established.

In addition, a great deal more must be known about individual response to natural hazards. In economic theory, the normative models for decision making under conditions of uncertainty assume that the individual seeks to maximize his expected gains or to minimize his expected losses based upon perceived probabilities. But studies of response to uncertainty suggest that there is a general tendency for decision makers to construct highly simplified models of the real world. It appears that emphasis is placed upon attaining adaptive levels of achievement rather than maximization *per se*. Alternative models of decision making are being developed that stress the limitations of man's ability to process information and to deal with uncertainty. It seems clear that people do not usually employ the principles of probability theory in estimating the outcomes of uncertain events.[1] How will they respond to a change in expected probabilities following a prediction? Research is needed to increase the understanding of private and public decision processes that determine adjustments for earthquakes and earthquake prediction.

We cannot wait for the experience records of several predictions to test hypotheses concerning regional economic behavior. As the first regional seismic networks are being installed, it would be possible to design and construct at least one regional economic model of an area monitored for precursory signs. Such a pilot model would permit the simulations of various assumptions about the behavior of businesses, households, and agencies in response to a prediction and the simulation of this behavior over the period prior to the quake. It would also be possible to simulate alternative public policies for predisaster aid and to see their effects on the economy. The seismic considerations would require extensive modeling of land-use patterns and spatial linkages within the region. Experience gained in the construction of pilot models would allow us to make more reliable predictions about economic effects of predictions and various types of predisaster policies to follow.

ECONOMIC DISRUPTION

One of the central concerns of officials concerning the issuance of an earthquake prediction is the possibility of panic reactions that might seriously disrupt the economic system. Here we refer to panic in the economic sense rather than the panic flight mentioned in Chapter 4. Would the economy be thrown into disorder? Would panic selling throw real estate and securities markets into chaos? As noted in the previous

[1] Paul Slovic, Howard Kunreuther, and Gilbert F. White, "Decision Processes, Rationality, and Adjustment to Natural Hazards," *Natural Hazards: Local, National, and Global,* Gilbert F. White (ed.) (New York: Oxford University Press, 1974), pp. 187–205.

chapter, it has even been suggested that the "prediction might be more devastating than the event."[2] In contrast, an economist[3] has argued that it is difficult to see why a reliable prediction with a long lead time should create panic.

There is at present no definitive answer to these contrasting points of view. All previous experience of regional reactions to bad news tends to support the view that the economy would not be thrown into panic.[4] Attempts to suppress information regarding the prediction could well generate rumors and lead to excessive speculative behavior. An open information policy to keep the public informed about a possible impending disaster would minimize the game of speculation. However, real estate and financial markets would probably reflect the new probabilities of possible future income losses and damages for properties at risk. A fall in market values of such assets would be a rational adjustment; although deplorable, it should be expected. As a way to reduce possible future loss, reduction in the levels of employment, production, and investment could be considered within extremely hazardous geographical areas. Transfer of vulnerable activities to other parts of the region or to other parts of the country might be a desirable long-run response. Alternatively, provision of disaster insurance, strengthening of structures, and other types of investment within the region could prove economical as a way to reduce losses.

Some economic relocation, some economic losses, and some economic disruption are inevitable. Policy makers should not be surprised at market discounting of expected future losses. Public policies for community preparedness to reduce earthquake hazards and public policies aiding the transition and supporting the level of income within the region could minimize the impact of the various adjustments to the expected event. Public assistance for the relocation of vulnerable activities, aid for the strengthening of structures, financial support for public utilities and local governments, the establishment of a program of federal earthquake insurance, and increased unemployment compensation would do a great deal to stabilize the economy and speed the adjustment process.

Federal aid given prior to an earthquake in order to lessen the negative

---

[2]Garrett Hardin, "Earthquakes: Prediction More Devastating Than Events," *Stalking the Wild Taboo* (Los Altos, California: William Kaufmann, Inc., 1973), pp. 123–134.

[3]Personal correspondence with Jack Hirshleifer, University of California, Los Angeles, August 13, 1974.

[4]For example, the economy of Britain adjusted to the news of the German blitz with little apparent disorganization. Perhaps the stabilizing influences can be attributed in part to the belief that losses would be widespread and that government aid would be available to those who suffered losses.

economic consequences of earthquake warnings may well be less costly than traditional postdisaster relief and rehabilitation. Yet with the advent of long lead times it is clear that the region itself will have to bear part of the cost of adjustment. Care will have to be taken that predisaster aid policies provide incentives to reduce possible losses. Well-meaning but ill-advised attempts to stabilize the regional economy could provide incentives for businesses or residents to stay in hazardous areas without taking steps to reduce risk. In general, aid should be tied to concomitant measures to reduce risks, such as strengthening buildings or removing potentially dangerous parts of buildings.

PREDICTION FAILURES

No earthquake prediction system will be foolproof. There will probably be failures to predict as well as incorrect predictions. Local public officials have reason to be concerned about the economic and political consequences of prediction failures. Each type of error will have different probabilities and different economic consequences.

The costs of a failure to predict will be the difference between the losses from an unanticipated earthquake and the losses of an anticipated quake plus the costs of adjustment measures. It is possible that the presence of a warning system, even though imperfect, will increase the losses from an unanticipated quake if it causes businesses and households to take more risks. (Of course, by alerting people to the earthquake risk, it may have the opposite effect.) The costs of an incorrect prediction would be difficult to specify because of several possibilities: No quake occurs at all; a quake occurs at the wrong place or time; or a quake occurs with a different magnitude from that predicted. All predictions will induce some costs of extra protection and some economic disruption. No immediate benefits accrue unless the quake occurs, although some of the adjustments made may be of benefit in dealing with possible future quakes.

Public officials will be concerned about economic costs incurred by the region when prediction proves incorrect or when there is a failure to predict. The economic losses will in turn change the political climate as blame is placed upon the public sector. For private firms and households, we are unable at present to say how many false alarms would destroy the credibility of an otherwise credible prediction. Disbelief and skepticism may increase the long-run costs of future predicted quakes. Attitudes toward risk bearing may be more a function of past experience in successful forecasting than of the probability attached to a particular prediction.

THE PRIVATE SECTOR

The greatest economic gains and costs from earthquake prediction occur in the private sector. Economic consequences of prediction can be estimated only in relation to the economic base of the region affected by the prediction. We must start with a clear picture of the sources and levels of income and employment for the community and the region. Economic projections for the prequake period should pay attention to local supply factors as well as to the demand side of the economy. The analysis of demand should specify those businesses whose sales are primarily outside the region (export industries) and those businesses whose sales are tied to the level of local income and employment (local industries). It is quite possible that local industries may be harder hit than export industries during the prequake period. Much of this depends upon whether the export industries decide to relocate their plants outside the region.

Additional demand sectors of the economy are business investment, housing investment, government investment, and current government operations. Each of these sectors will be affected differently by the initial prediction and by subsequent reactions to the initial decisions made by officials in office at that time. The chain of economic reactions cannot be easily visualized without a picture of the input–output relations between the industries *within* the region and the demand and supply linkages *to* other regions. If declines occur in the demand sectors because businesses leave the area or if decreases in demand occur because investments within the region decline, there will be downward multiplier effects on local income and employment. It is likely that total local income and employment will fall by a multiple of the original decrease in demand, e.g., perhaps by a factor of 1.6 with a 6-month lag, depending on the structure of the local economy and the size and source of the original decrease in demand.

The reactions of major banks, lending institutions, and insurance companies that conduct business in the region are especially important. Their actions will be influenced by federal insurance and aid policies. In the absence of federal policies to provide some predisaster financial support and an inflow of public funds, the private funds market may become very tight. Standby federal predisaster policies to cushion the potential impact of a sudden tightening of credit would probably be desirable. If public predisaster policies are established and known in advance, economic reactions within the region may be considerably milder than if the region is hit with a prediction without any published predisaster policy.

All financial firms will review portfolio holdings and re-examine borrowing and lending policies. New loans for properties at risk will reflect the probability of damage. For some properties it may be difficult to get any loans at all from private lenders. The size of loans and the interest rate charged for risky enterprises and properties will reflect the new expected probabilities of loss brought about by the prediction. Some enterprises will suffer if their sales are tied to the level of regional income, even though they may not have properties at risk.

A study of the possible flight of funds from the region would be desirable. The outflow of funds may be a rational response, given the new probabilities of risk within the region. However, rational responses by financial institutions may or may not be desirable from a regional point of view. Again, predisaster public policy will be crucial in seeing that orderly adjustments are followed. The inflow of public funds can offset in large part the outflow of private funds. Inflows of public funds in themselves may do little good, however, if they do not provide incentives for recipients to take actions to reduce risk and reduce the hazard potential.

It is clear that different groups in the region will react with different speeds. Securities and real estate markets may quickly register declines in businesses and properties where the probabilities of loss are high. The markets will also register some increases for businesses and properties within and outside the region where competitive advantage has increased as a result of the prediction. Market changes will reflect speculative transactions as well as the discounting of technological losses. By contrast, small firms and households may wait for more information and not take action until strong public action is evident or until they are affected by the decisions of large firms and financial institutions. The income and employment multiplier effects of the first reactions to the prediction may take some months to work themselves out. We might expect to see declines in personal incomes and a rise in regional unemployment rates within six months to a year following a prediction. Businesses that have a large economic stake in the region will analyze the returns and costs of the various adjustments open to them while buying more information and advice from private seismologists, engineering firms, and market-research agencies.

The demand for new housing investment and business construction will probably be weakened by the prediction. It is evident that there will be a demand to strengthen many types of structures and to build up some kinds of inventories. The strength of this demand will depend upon the availability of funds in the money market as a whole and the financial reserve position of businesses and households. By contrast, the desire to postpone durable investments subject to possible damage will be strong. New housing starts and construction permits would be expected to decline and remain down until after the expected quake.

It is plausible to argue that individual households and small businesses may react only passively to the local economic situation and that the reactions of influential decision makers will really govern. Yet small businesses and households may be more averse to taking risks; this attitude could lead to premature actions. For example, it is possible that speculators could encourage panic selling ("blockbusting" practices) or excessive and unneeded repairs of structures. Although it is likely that single-story, wood-frame structures will suffer relatively little damage from shaking, it is not clear that this is really believed by homeowners. It is also possible that homeowners in quake areas may tend to withhold mortgage payments as the time of the quake approaches. The rationale would be that financial institutions could not resell the properties because of expected damage and that they would thus feel it would be better to let the present occupants remain. After the quake, the homeowner could make up the back payments if the damages were nominal but might "walk away" in the event of severe damage. A different outcome would be expected if earthquake insurance were available.

The Insurance Problem

A special problem may result from the effect of a prediction upon the policies of insurance companies concerning *all* types of property insurance—not just earthquake insurance—in the region. There appears to be an important difference between the patterns of ownership in financial markets and insurance markets. For example, if a stockholder owns a claim on the proceeds of an enterprise when a prediction is made, he will bear the loss of the fall in expected future income. When risks are insured by insurance companies, the pattern of ownership is reversed. In this case the business firm has a contingent claim upon the insurance company to cover the risk. However, in the case of property insurance this claim is periodically renewed and is therefore revocable:

> There is a question [of] who should bear the capital loss associated with the forecasts of disaster. Should the insurer bear the loss, just as he bears it if the disaster occurs without having been foreseen? Or should the insurer be permitted to withdraw his obligation, and make the enterprise bear the loss? It seems to me that there is no answer to this dilemma. It can only be resolved by making the possibility of a forecast an explicit or implicit part of the contract of insurance.[5]

---

[5]Personal correspondence with John M. Marshall, Assistant Professor of Economics, University of California, Santa Barbara, October 3, 1974.

This matter is important because both lending institutions, which require insurance on mortgaged properties, and the typical insurance buyer tend to believe that the property is insured. By contrast, it would be possible for insurance companies to exercise outlet clauses in the contracts and not to renew policies as they came due during the long lead time prior to the quake. The problem of insurability is explicitly acknowledged in disability and life insurance. Apparently, this concept has not been extended to property insurance.

It might be argued that this conclusion is not realistic. Although insurance companies have the legal right to refuse to renew policies on commercial and residential structures when an earthquake prediction is made for a given area, in fact they probably won't. On political and public-relations grounds, it would be costly for a company to cancel policies. With a long-term prediction, e.g., 10 years, insurance companies would probably attempt not to take on new business, but even this step would create political problems. Companies would undoubtedly request rate increases. It is likely that state insurance commissioners would deny the requests. In effect, the rates for insurance would be frozen. Perhaps lapsed policies would not be renewed. Insured property that was sold might not be reinsured for the new owner. But insurance companies would probably find it necessary to continue insurance for policyholders who hold insurance at the time of the prediction. Nevertheless, it is clear that the establishment of earthquake prediction may seriously weaken the use of private insurance (as it exists today) as a way of reducing costs associated with natural disaster.

Current insurance policies for property insurance are based upon the law of large numbers and the pooling of reserves. Damages in the case of earthquakes are interdependent, and there is a problem of adverse risk selection for an entire region. The issuance of a prediction of a serious quake may serve to make it clear that reserves based upon the law of large numbers may not be adequate. This will be particularly important for common types of property insurance such as fire and extended-coverage insurance, which greatly exceed the amount of coverage of earthquake insurance. Extension of the guarantee of insurability to property subject to earthquake hazards is important. Yet this extension will be difficult for insurance companies unless they are enabled to offer insurance for risks where the law of large numbers does not apply. It can be argued that government reinsurance would be helpful here. Another argument that can be made is that insurance of catastrophic losses from disasters cannot be handled well by the *reserves principle* but is much better dealt with by insurance based upon the *mutuality principle*.[6]

[6] John M. Marshall, "Insurance Theory: Reserves Versus Mutuality," *Economic Inquiry*, 12 (December 1974), 476–492.

The availability of insurance affects not only the workings of real estate and financial markets but also the value of other types of damage mitigation. It may be desirable from a social point of view to substitute some form of insurance for other forms of damage mitigation as a means of protection against losses. That is to say, it may be socially desirable to substitute insurance for the transfer of vulnerable activities away from the region or the strengthening of structures. The availability of insurance may thus prevent overexpenditure on other means of loss reduction.

The entire question of the feasibility of insurance as a means of protection against earthquake hazards needs further study.[7] In addition to the question of providing insurance coverage for natural disasters, there are other important questions. Fire insurance is now required by most lending institutions. Should disaster insurance be similarly made compulsory? Should disaster insurance be comprehensive, i.e., covering all natural hazards? How should premiums be determined prior to a prediction and after a prediction? Are public subsidies for disaster insurance justified? Is there a practical way of insuring economic losses other than physical damages, such as general income losses? What would be the effect on the mortgage industry and real estate markets if insurance companies did not renew property-damage insurance after the announcement of an earthquake prediction?

THE PUBLIC SECTOR

Finally, the path of economic activity will have parallel effects upon public utilities, public agencies, and local governments. If local property values fall and the economy dips, property- and sales-tax revenues, accounting for more than two thirds of local public revenues, will decline. At the same time, high levels of public services (schools, streets and roads, health and hospitals, and public welfare) should be maintained, and some functions (emergency agencies, strengthening of public structures, and fire protection) should be expanded. How can local public services be maintained and expanded in the face of falling revenues? Some new public construction should be postponed. Yet other types of public construction should be increased. How will local public agencies maintain repayment and interest schedules on existing debt? How will new public debt be financed if regional capital markets are tightened pending the expected quake? If tax incentives are provided to local prop-

---

[7]Howard Kunreuther, "Disaster Insurance: A Tool for Hazard Mitigation," *Journal of Risk and Insurance,* 41 (June 1974), 287– 303.

erty owners to engage in strengthening of structures, who will make up for the loss in tax revenues?

In many ways, the plight of public utilities will be similar to that of local governments. They will have demands to maintain service levels and to undertake investment in hazard reduction at the same time that their revenues may be falling and their ability to borrow may be impaired.

There are no obvious answers to all these questions. What types of federal aid for the predisaster and postdisaster periods can best encourage needed adjustments, stabilize the economy, and address the serious problem of equity among groups that bear a disproportionate share of the cost? To what extent should the taxpayers of other regions be liable for hazard reduction in earthquake-prone areas? We must have a comprehensive disaster policy that deals extensively with predisaster adjustments as well as one that is directed toward relief and recovery.

INFORMATION THEORY, FOREKNOWLEDGE, AND LEVELS OF ADJUSTMENT

From the viewpoint of economic theory, the ability to make credible predictions of an impending earthquake can be treated as a problem in the theory of information. The information supplied by an earthquake prediction is a case of what has been referred to as foreknowledge.[8] Private foreknowledge (inside information about an earthquake prediction) can lead to redistributive gains that have no social value. Public information (information known to all) can result in production and consumption decisions that are socially desirable. The social value of foreknowledge with respect to earthquakes will increase with its certainty, general diffusion, applicability, content, and decision relevance. Clearly, great care should be taken to see that the information is given wide dissemination. Also, the social value of the prediction will be enhanced by the supply of additional information on appropriate responses by businesses, households, and public agencies and by the provision of incentives to encourage particular kinds of responses, e.g., public grants and loans.

In addition to the social value of the information, there will likely be redistributive and pecuniary gains (as opposed to technological gains of productive adaptation) accruing to people and firms able to speculate and make trades at the expense of others. The net economic value of

---

[8]Jack Hirshleifer, "The Private and Social Value of Information and the Reward for Inventive Activity," *American Economic Review*, 61 (September 1971), 561–574.

these redistributions will be zero—i.e., the sum of gains will equal the sum of the losses. However, there may be some undesirable equity effects on the distribution of income. To the extent that the prediction is prematurely released to insiders, to the extent that the diffusion and dissemination of the information are imperfect, to the extent that there are market imperfections, and to the extent that different groups can buy superior information through private predictions, it will be possible for speculators to gain at the expense of others through market transactions.

Speculators, having taken a position, may find it desirable to resell information or to spend resources to "push" information[9] It is possible that such dissemination of information through private channels can shift prices that lead to productive adaptations. Yet it is clear that gains from speculation may give rise to the socially wasteful dissemination of information.

Before a prediction, the normal probability would dictate that a certain amount of current resources be devoted to earthquake-reduction practices. Costly programs to achieve high levels of protection would be held in abeyance. It is generally wise to defer emergency costs and to utilize resources in other ways when probabilities are very low. Once an emergency prediction is made, it will be desirable to engage in crash programs to achieve higher levels of protection.

To summarize, before a prediction there will exist for a seismic region some low probability that a strong quake might occur. After the initial prediction, the normal period is succeeded by an emergency period extending until the quake occurs or the prediction is withdrawn. When new information is provided, as the prediction is subsequently updated, the probabilities will be revised accordingly. During the emergency period, productive adjustments will be made and market prices will adjust to reflect the impending disaster. Some crash emergency programs will become economical. Market imperfections and the uneven diffusion of information about the prediction and how to react to it will cause many traders to take speculative positions. Attempts will be made to "push" information to enhance speculative positions. The optimal level of adjustment would be one that minimized the sum of the adjustment costs plus the residual damages to be sustained.

ESTIMATING BENEFITS AND COSTS OF ADJUSTMENTS

Comprehensive benefit–cost studies of the various means to reduce earthquake hazards do not presently exist even for relatively static condi-

[9] *Ibid.*

tions. Existing earthquake-damage estimates are of three types: estimates of damages from past quakes; annualized loss estimates based upon expected probabilities of events per year of a certain intensity; and the sudden loss estimates for unanticipated quakes in various urban areas at various times in the future.

By and large, loss estimates for earthquakes in the United States are based primarily upon property damages. To structural damages are added damages to contents of buildings, and adjustments are made for lives lost and for injuries sustained. No estimates are made of regional income losses that are not related to direct damages.

Several economic criticisms can be made of current methods for estimating earthquake damages. First, many properties will fall in value because the economic system has been damaged even though the properties themselves will not be damaged. Second, not all income losses suffered by property owners and others will be reflected in the decline in property values. Third, it is not correct to compare losses in 1970 with those in 1980, 1990, or 2000 without discounting them in terms of present values.

Cochrane[10] has been one of the first to recognize that concentration on average annual damages or direct damages to property and life may not take into account total damages to the regional economic system. He used an input–output model to forecast the economic impact of an 8.3-magnitude earthquake occurring in San Francisco in 1974. He found direct damages to structures of $7 billion (using traditional methods for property-damage estimation), and to this figure he added $6 billion for a loss of value added to the gross regional product, for a total of 13 billion in damages. However, there are two major grounds on which to question these estimates. First, the damage to property is a function of the loss of its income-producing potential. Hence, adding together property damages and income lost clearly involves some degree of double counting. Second, none of the earthquake-damage studies to date notes that damages to a region which may reduce economic activity locally, may *not* be losses from the standpoint of the nation as a whole. If there is excess capacity elsewhere in the national economic system, reductions in income and employment locally may be offset by increases in income and employment elsewhere.

In summary, current procedures for loss estimation have serious economic limitations. Some of the common errors are failure to discount

---

[10]Harold C. Cochrane, "Predicting the Economic Impact of Earthquakes," *Social Science Perspectives on the Coming San Francisco Earthquake: Economic Impact, Prediction, and Reconstruction,* Natural Hazard Research Working Paper No. 25 (Boulder, Colorado: University of Colorado Institute of Behavioral Science, 1974), pp. 1–39.

costs and benefits having different time dimensions, double counting, failure to make proper estimates of nonproperty losses, confusion between regional and national effects, and aggregation of damages to economic subsystems without looking at the regional economic system as a whole. Until we have better procedures for estimating losses and costs of adjustment, we will be on uncertain ground in estimating benefits and costs of alternative ways to reduce earthquake hazards.

SELECTED REFERENCES

Cochrane, Harold C. "Predicting the Economic Impact of Earthquakes," *Social Science Perspectives on the Coming San Francisco Earthquake: Economic Impact, Prediction, and Reconstruction,* Natural Hazard Research Working Paper No. 25. Boulder, Colorado: University of Colorado Institute of Behavioral Science, 1974. pp. 1–39.

Dacy, Douglas C., and Howard Kunreuther. *The Economics of Natural Disasters.* New York: The Free Press, 1969.

Hirshleifer, Jack. "The Private and Social Value of Information and the Reward for Inventive Activity," *American Economic Review,* 61 (September 1971), 561–574.

Hirshleifer, Jack. "Where Are We In The Theory of Information," *American Economic Review,* LXIII (May 1973).

Kunreuther, Howard. "Disaster Insurance: A Tool for Hazard Mitigation," *Journal of Risk and Insurance,* 41 (June 1974), 287–303.

Kunreuther, Howard. *Recovery from Natural Disasters: Insurance or Federal Aid,* Washington, D.C.' American Enterprise Institute, December 1973.

Marshall, John M. "Insurance Theory: Reserves Versus Mutuality," *Economic Inquiry,* 12 (December 1974), 476–492.

Marshall, John M. "Private Incentives and Public Information," *American Economic Review,* LXIV (June 1974).

McClure, Frank. *Studies in Gathering Earthquake Damage Statistics.* Coast and Geodetic Survey, U.S. Department of the Interior. Washington, D.C.: U.S. Government Printing Office, 1967.

National Oceanic and Atmospheric Administration, U.S. Department of Commerce. *A Study of Earthquake Losses in the Los Angeles, California Area.* Washington, D.C.: U.S. Government Printing Office, 1973.

National Oceanic and Atmospheric Administration, U.S. Department of Commerce. *A Study of Earthquake Losses in the San Francisco Bay Area.* Washington, D.C.: U.S. Government Printing Office, 1972.

Russell, Clifford S. "Losses from Natural Hazards," *Land Economics,* 46 (November 1970), 383–393.

Slovic, Paul, Howard Kunreuther, and Gilbert F. White. "Decision Processes, Rationality, and Adjustment to Natural Hazards," *Natural Hazards: Local, National, and Global,* Gilbert F. White (ed.) New York: Oxford University Press, 1974. pp. 187–205.

Wiggins Co., J. H. *Budgeting Justification for Earthquake Engineering Research,* Technical Report 74-1201-1. Redondo Beach, California: J. H. Wiggins Co., May 10, 1974.

6 Legal Implications of Earthquake Prediction

Throughout this report, we have stressed the unique characteristics of earthquakes and earthquake predictions. Unlike other disasters, earthquakes are not preceded by any generally observable phenomena. Neither the public nor the scientific community completely understands the potential for devastation from earthquakes or from the events they trigger. Despite this lack of understanding, however, we are on the threshold of possessing the capability to predict accurately the locale and magnitude of some earthquakes months or years in advance. Such predictions would enable the institution of hazard-reduction programs that could save thousands of lives. Credible predictions will also elicit responses that might damage social and economic systems in the threatened areas.

These unique qualities make it impossible to provide definitive answers to the legal issues raised by earthquake predictions. Clearly, the development of a prediction capability will require some modifications in the existing concepts of social responsibility. The nature of the modifications will depend upon: (a) the indirect and direct social responses to earthquake predictions and (b) the types and expected effectiveness of the hazard-reduction measures used.

PREDICTION-RELATED LIABILITY

Subject to the stated qualifications, which may induce modifications of existing concepts of responsibility, some premises regarding earthquake-prediction-related liability can be offered with a fair degree of confidence. We assume that the early legally significant predictions will originate with a relatively small group of qualified scientists employed in the private and public sectors. We further assume that the scientifically based predictions will be offered as expressions of opinion, that they will be accompanied by supportive data upon which they are based, and that they will be carefully qualified as to the degree of reliability accorded a prediction by its originators, often expressed in terms of probability percentages.

PUBLICIZING PREDICTIONS

Given these assumptions, scientists who provide public notice of their prediction—whether it turns out to be correct or incorrect—should not, under existing legal principles, incur any valid risks of liability to those who may suffer damage or injury resulting from the prediction. Nor should the public media expect to incur liability as a consequence of publicizing the prediction, so long as reasonable care is taken to avoid inaccurate statements and to avoid deliberate stimulation of public anxiety for self-serving purposes.

DELAYING PUBLIC DISCLOSURE

If the initial disclosure is made only to appropriate public officials who then attempt to postpone public disclosure from a justifiable desire to prevent premature and detrimental public responses,[1] a conflict of opinion might provoke individual disclosure to mass media personnel, followed by efforts to enjoin publication of the disclosed information. Situations might arise under which the courts could be persuaded to enjoin publication of a prediction temporarily; however, both the current state of the law and present judicial and societal attitudes make such a situation unlikely.

If public disclosure were made, public officials who felt the disclosure was unwarranted or potentially detrimental might try to discredit the prediction or launch personal attacks on the scientist–predictors. Given sufficient time, planning, and awareness of legal vulnerabilities, public officials might successfully carry out either effort with relative impunity. Offsetting factors might include the low credibility sometimes accorded public officials, countermeasures taken by an indignant scientific com-

---

[1]In Chapters 1 and 4 and elsewhere in this volume we urge that predictions be released directly to the public by the scientists involved.

munity, and the capacity of the communication media to ferret out and bring all the facts to public attention. Any such furor would of itself provide the very publicity that officials sought to avoid. However, it would leave the public uncertain as to the degree of credibility to give to the prediction, would reduce confidence in any subsequent earthquake-protection programs, and would impose delays on further evaluation and institution of hazard-reduction programs. Thus, public officials should be provided in advance with the best possible analyses of the detrimental and beneficial consequences to be expected from publicizing a prediction or issuing a warning, and a procedure for receiving, evaluating, and publicizing predictions and issuing warnings should be established as soon as possible.

Without such a procedure, the public would benefit little from bringing public officials to account for malfeasance. But we should not ignore the responsibility they carry for avoiding the issuance of unwarranted earthquake warnings, since serious detrimental consequences could evolve as a direct consequence of the warning. It is conceivable that premature and unwarranted predictions might be announced in an effort to influence the acquisition of further financial support, or even to achieve desired notoriety, and that supportive data could be so manipulated as to appear more conclusive than they actually are.

The best time to deal with such possibilities is while the earthquake-prediction capability is in an embryonic state, not after the first potentially destructive earthquake is predicted for a heavily populated area.

Failure to disclose an authenticated prediction could lead to successful claims for compensation for deprivations that could have been avoided had the prediction not been deliberately withheld by those possessing the necessary information. If the failure to disclose were attributable to governmental agencies, malfeasance or misfeasance in office might be invoked as a basis for claiming compensation. The shorter the lead time inherent in the prediction, the stronger the possibilities of successful claims based on failure to disclose. Currently, the uncertainty of prediction capabilities and the existing state of the law render the chances of a successful claim negligible. Ten or twenty years hence such a possibility may become valid.

If government personnel are found negligent with respect to publication or suppression of a prediction, the initial burden to be overcome by a petitioner derives from the doctrine of sovereign immunity. This doctrine has been eroded to varying degrees by case law, from jurisdiction to jurisdiction, and has been abrogated to a substantial degree by legislative prescription in some. But the doctrine remains, and there is a considerable degree of uncertainty—even under the Federal Tort Claims Act or similar state legislation such as the California Tort Claims Act[2]—with respect to the existence and extent of the immunity. Matters falling within the discretionary powers of government are not actionable (i.e., not cause for legal action), but the dividing line between exercise of discretionary powers and negligent implementation of decisions made under discretionary powers is shrouded by uncertainty.

PREDICTIONS THAT ARE PROVED ERRONEOUS

Another liability question concerns the consequences of predictions that are proved erroneous by either the failure of a predicted earthquake to occur or the accumulation and evaluation of contradictory data. If the original prediction had been accorded a high degree of credibility by the scientific community, by officials, by the media, and by the public, a number of irreversible prediction-responsive decisions would have been made and acted upon, many of which imposed direct or consequential deprivations on various groups of people within the threatened locality. Here, too, under existing legal principles, a prediction that carried the qualifications already stated would probably not serve as a basis for judicial assessments of liability. Prospective complainants would have to carry a heavy burden of proof. They would have to establish a substantial degree of negligence[3] pertaining to the original prediction, to prove reasonable detrimental reliance on the prediction, to establish a direct causative chain between prediction and deprivation, to demonstrate the foreseeability of the deprivation, to prove actual damages, and to establish a bar to such recognized defenses as contributory negligence. While the emphasis on each of these requirements might vary from one jurisdiction to another, they would be well-nigh insurmountable in most. It is also possible that such claims might be barred by statutes of limitations, although the courts might hold that such statutes did not become applicable until the complainant could have become aware that his deprivation resulted from an erroneous prediction. This would not happen until the predicted event failed to occur when expected.

In the absence of any demonstration of negligence on the part of government, existing legal principles and precedents would preclude tort liability for governmentally issued earthquake predictions or warnings that proved erroneous. (Political vulnerability would be another matter.) If actionable negligence were established, the master-servant relationship

[2]The uncertainty with regard to the California Tort Claims Act is evidenced in the 1972 case of *Nestle* v. *City of Santa Monica.* See *California Reporter,* 101 (1972), 568.
[3]Rules as to actionable (i.e., cause for legal action) negligence and as to defenses of comparative or contributory negligence vary from jurisdiction to jurisdiction.

would prevent the shifting of liability to government officials, though under some circumstances they could be found jointly and severally liable along with the governmental agency in whose service they acted. A remote possibility exists that their acts would be so clearly *ultra vires* (i.e., beyond the scope of their legal power) that the officials alone could be found responsible, but such a potential is probably not present within the context of earthquake prediction as the process is presently envisioned.

SUMMARY

In summary, existing legal principles include a presumption that no liability can be attributed to foreseeable consequences of responsible earthquake prediction activities. Whether that presumption will weaken in the future or whether, under some circumstances, specific liability should be prescribed, is a proper subject for further evaluation based on the unique aspects of earthquake prediction. When such evaluations are made, the practical consequences of legal actions should receive careful attention. The 8 years required for a judicial determination with respect to federal liability under the Federal Tort Claims Act in the aftermath of the Texas City disaster of 1946 largely nullified the purpose of restoring the plaintiffs as nearly as possible to their prior condition.[4] The criminal prosecution of the designing engineers following the Vaiont dam disaster in Italy was even less beneficial.[5]

LAND-USE CONTROLS

In making an initial assessment of the legal aspects of earthquake prediction, one is obliged to look beyond the prediction itself to representative responses that it will elicit. One of the most important potential benefits from an earthquake prediction with a long lead time could be the chance to use land-use management and control procedures in reducing the earthquake hazard. This benefit may not be realized, however, especially with the first predictions, because a long time will be consumed in surmounting the legal barriers to application of land-use management and control techniques. The total process may take more than 10 years, since the legal hurdles are rooted in the traditional constitution-based protections of individual property rights.

To demonstrate adequately the reasoning behind this contention is

---

[4]"*Dalehite* v. *United States,*" *U.S. Reports,* 346 (1953), 15.
[5]James M. Brown, "Beyond the Law and the Lab in Search of Public Safety Design Criteria," *Public Safety: A Growing Factor in Modern Design,* National Academy of Engineering (Washington, D.C.: National Academy of Sciences, 1970), pp. 16, 18.

impossible in the space available here. The following examples are intended, therefore, to be illustrative and are cursory in nature. They are based on the assumption that a prediction has been issued with a 10-year lead time preceding a 1-year time window and that 1 year of the 10 is consumed by the process of governmental verification of the prediction and a consequent decision to apply land-use control processes for hazard-reduction purposes.

OBSTACLES TO EMPLOYING LAND-USE CONTROLS

The traditional land-use control processes available are zoning, subdivision regulation, and building and housing codes (all of which fall under the inherent police-power regulatory processes of government) and the sovereign power of eminent domain (under which private property may be taken for public use if just compensation is paid). To the extent that police-power regulations are properly imposed, no compensation is required. The arrangements relating to compensable takings (or, under some state constitutions, including that of California, compensable damaging) of private property, and noncompensable regulation or restrictions upon *use* of private property, create difficulties in land-use management and control. The distinction between the limiting parameters of the power to regulate and the power to condemn is not a finely drawn line of demarcation but rather a large gray area of uncertainty, subject to specific definition on a case-by-case basis, reflecting far-ranging policy influences and fluctuating concepts of the rights of private property. Whatever these rights may be, they are zealously guarded by the courts. The opinion of Justice Holmes in *Pennsylvania Coal Co.* v. *Mahon*[6] in 1922, a landmark case reflecting this judicial attitude, is echoed in the recent case of *United States* v. *Reserve Mining Company*.[7]

Simply worded, the basic limitation of the police power is that its valid exercise must be a reasonable means to a legitimate end.[8] A legitimate end to be pursued within a program intended to reduce earthquake-related hazards would certainly be the protection and preservation of life and limb. An obvious threat to life and limb would surely be posed by buildings that could not withstand seismic stress. Logically, then, one might turn to the building codes as the focal point for regulatory actions de-

[6]*"Pennsylvania Coal Co.* v. *Mahon," U.S. Reports,* 260 (1922), 393.
[7]*"United States* v. *Reserve Mining Company," Federal Supplement Second Series,* 380, 11; injunction stayed, *Federal Reporter Second Series,* 498, 1073 (8th Circuit Court); application to vacate stay order denied, *Supreme Court Reporter,* 95 (1974), 287.
[8]See, e.g., *"Lawton* v. *Steele," U.S. Reports,* 152 (1894), 133; *Goldblatt* v. *Town of Hempstead," U.S. Reports* 369 (1962), 590.

Legal Implications of Earthquake Prediction 87

signed to eliminate or reduce risks imposed by structurally inadequate buildings. But before this step is taken, detailed standards (preferably of the performance type, though the older specification type prevails in many local jurisdictions) must be provided with respect to reduction of those hazards pertinent to earthquake-protection goals. Maximizing this potential will require incorporation of the latest advances in quake-proofing of structures into the standards to be applied, plus legislative determination of the extent to which such standards can and should be applied. Before sound decisions based on adequate information can be reached, a survey of existing buildings will be desirable. Such a survey, if sufficiently extensive, could be accompanied by specific recommendations to owners and occupants regarding the major risks to occupants and to passers-by.

Some potential legal impediments to the accomplishment of such an inspection and assessment program exist. Those who foresee imposition of costly building modification requirements may adopt the tactic of challenging inspector entry in order to at least delay such assessments.[9] Ultimately, such challenges will fail, but carelessly drawn legislation may first have to be rewritten. Similarly, the standards may be challenged under a void-for-vagueness contention, which often carries with it a reasonable chance of success in the litigation lottery.

Because present prediction capabilities do not permit a finely drawn delineation of the area at risk, the geographical area initially designated as vulnerable will be large and will include a number of local jurisdictions. In most instances each jurisdiction would have its own building code promulgation powers, delegated by the state. Uniform code modification and inspection certification processes are not likely to be adopted. Some initial legislative efforts would probably prove vulnerable to judicial challenges, which could at least delay the effective implementation of protective building codes in some sectors of the designated vulnerable area.

After the necessary surveys have been accomplished and the legislative decisions made regarding necessary code modifications, inspections would have to be based on the performance standards prescribed, and modification orders would result. Application of standards could also be subjected to judicial challenges, which would impose further delay in implementing protection programs. Modification orders would surely be challenged, in some instances through class action suits, on the basis that they constituted a partial or complete taking of private property for public use, thus requiring the payment of just compensation. Such "inverse

---

[9]Property and income tax rewards might dampen resistance to such impositions, however.

condemnation"[10] actions could easily fall into the gray area between clearly recognized regulatory power limits and condemnation. When property owners initiating such complaints are successful, the defendant municipalities may be assessed the costs of plaintiffs' attorney fees, appraiser fees, and so on, as well as the condemnation award itself. Such contests would probably be carried to appellate levels by the losing party. Before final resolution was achieved, several years could pass by. While such actions were pending, the defendant government could not push ahead with its enforcement program unless it were prepared to carry the judicially compounded costs in case the program were held to constitute a compensable taking.

Obviously, many of these issues would eventually be resolved judicially, at least in principle, with reliable precedents established, and with litigation-tested code models available for later use. Later earthquake predictions would be much less vulnerable to harassment. But the early prediction-response efforts could be subjected to such prolonged delays that by the time legal challenges were resolved and comprehensive building-code-related measures were enacted, the remaining lead time might be insufficient to accomplish any significant hazard reduction. A program initially designed to be accomplished in 7 or 8 years, if compressed into half that time or less, would be vulnerable to completely different amortization schedules, financing potentials, labor and material availabilities, compliance and enforcement processes, and perhaps to new taking challenges based on the shrunken compliance period allowable.

Similar challenges could be expected with respect to the other traditional land-use management and control processes.

BUILDING CODES AND EXISTING STRUCTURES

Building codes traditionally have been limited in application to buildings yet to be constructed. If a building is constructed in full compliance with code requirements in force at the time the building permit is issued, it must be accepted as in compliance with the code, and an occupancy permit must be issued upon completion even if the code is changed during construction. Subsequent code modifications, with which the building does not comply, are not applicable retroactively. This aspect is more crippling to the hazard-reduction prospects than all the other impediments previously mentioned. We have already mentioned (Chapter 3)

[10]Under such a cause of action, the complainant alleges that regulatory efforts go beyond police-power limits and in fact constitute a taking or condemnation of complainant's property.

that 40,000 buildings in Los Angeles County alone do not conform to quake-resistance standards enacted after the Long Beach earthquake of 1933. The San Fernando earthquake of 1971 taught many new lessons regarding structural earthquake vulnerabilities that should now be incorporated into building codes to assure that necessary safety features will be reflected in the design of future buildings and other structures.

One solution may be a two-step code provision. It may be structurally and economically feasible to design buildings to satisfy minimal earthquake-resistance standards and also to incorporate into them a capacity to accommodate the temporary addition of further reinforcement at some later date. With such a design potential available, a building code could impose, as a prerequisite to issuance of a building permit, a requirement that the owner incorporate into the building provisions for accommodating supplemental reinforcement components. Within a specified period after the building was identified as being within an officially designated earthquake-prediction locality, the code could require that reinforcements be added or the occupancy permit surrendered. Such a two-step code could allow a lesser degree of earthquake-resistant capacity to be required for buildings in general, thus helping to hold down costs, while assuring that a greater seismic-stress-resistant capability would be added in localities where an official earthquake warning has been issued.

This type of postconstruction application of a building-code provision should withstand legal challenge because the owner had agreed to it in exchange for being relieved of the obligation of incorporating the maximum code-provided seismic-stress reinforcement requirements at the time of initial construction. This demonstrates the possible benefits and flexibilities that may be derived from the capacity to predict earthquakes with a considerable degree of specificity, as well as the potentials that may be realized when experts from different fields collaborate in attacking earthquake hazard-reduction problems.

HOUSING CODES

Housing codes, also developed to further public health and safety, have not been considered to be subject to the "prospective application only" constraints that limit building-code potentials, because they merely impose requirements for the continuation of certain specified uses of a structure. Such restrictions have generally been conceded to be within the bounds of police-power regulation. Housing codes have been directed primarily at residential leasehold properties, though other specific health and safety codes exist in most communities.[11] Retroactive applications of housing codes have generally avoided constitutional taking challenges because they do not, in theory, proscribe *all* uses of the property, but rather are directed to the prohibition of certain specified uses unless the buildings are brought into and maintained in compliance with the code-specified public health and safety standards.

As long as the standards imposed are reasonable, are fairly applied under equal protection prescriptions, and are in compliance with due-process requirements, they will withstand judicial challenge unless it is established that code compliance will in effect destroy all economic uses to which the property can reasonably be put. Even then, if a noncomplying building poses a clear and present danger to the casual public in its existing state, a building inspector may have the power to order an owner to bring the building into compliance with pertinent health and safety codes, or to have it razed.

As credible earthquake-prediction capability is achieved, new comprehensive earthquake-resistant-structural requirements might prove acceptable to the courts even when applied to existing buildings. If the lead time provided by the prediction is long enough to allow reasonable capitalization of the costs of required modification, retroactive application of standards might be justified under an amortization concept similar to that often incorporated into zoning codes in recent years. The logical position would require the modifications to be ordered upon the designation of a locality as vulnerable under an official earthquake warning and to be completed by a specified time prior to the date predicted as the start of the time window. Undoubtedly, such a legislative program would be subjected to judicial challenge. To the extent possible, such challenges should be made prior to the prediction, by means of friendly suits testing codes already promulgated and, where possible, by seeking declaratory judgments or at least attorney-general opinions.

The consequences of ordering a noncomplying building razed once the time window for the event has been entered, only to have the prediction demonstrated to be erroneous by the failure of the predicted earthquake to materialize, require further legal inquiry and investigation.

ZONING CODES AND SUBDIVISION REGULATIONS

Zoning codes and subdivision regulations generally operate only prospectively. In application they relate to a defined area rather than to

[11] For example, fire codes and codes imposing special safety conditions for hospitals, schools, and theaters.

specific parcels of land. Land uses rendered nonconforming by changes in zoning codes generally are allowed to continue until terminated by natural attrition, though on occasion the demise has been hurried along by amortization limitations establishing a legal deadline. However, amortization periods, if not based on reasonable useful-life expectancies, have been found to constitute a compensable taking.

Changes in existing zoning are limited by various interpretations of the permissible parameters of "original mistake or substantially changed conditions" rules. Where down-zoning of previously permitted uses has been attempted, it has sometimes been held by the courts to constitute at least a partial taking, requiring compensation for the resultant diminution in market value.

Subdivision regulations can make disclosure of known earthquake-risk exposures an essential prerequisite to validity of sales contracts and property transfers and can augment zoning limitations that deny certain uses known to be particularly vulnerable to specific hazards. For example, if the geologic propensities demonstrated in the Turnagain area of Anchorage, Alaska, had been foreseeable, such an area could have been restricted to recreational purposes, if included in a development project.[12]

New concepts of land-use management and control such as transferrable development rights, land banking, critical area designations, and compensatory regulation are being explored and experimented with today. The traditional land-use control mechanisms are currently being subjected to challenge on many fronts because they have allegedly failed to serve the societal functions expected and needed. The "quiet revolution in land-use control"[13] is far from running its course, and any earthquake-prediction analysis that failed to take into account the potentials inherent in this dynamic process would be censurably deficient.

REAL ESTATE MORTGAGE MARKETS

The possible effects of a long-term prediction on the real estate mortgage market raise many legal questions. Private mortgage lenders may be reluctant to make loans in areas where an earthquake has been predicted

---

[12]The Alaska earthquake of March 27, 1964, caused a large landslide in the Turnagain Heights coastline area near Anchorage. The ground motion of the quake caused the soils in the slide area to weaken and momentarily liquefy. Seventy-five houses in the 130-acre slide area were destroyed, and many more were damaged.
[13]Fred Bosselman and David Callies, *The Quiet Revolution in Land-Use Control,* Council on Environmental Quality (Washington, D.C.: U.S. Government Printing Office, 1971).

to occur, or they may require that new structures in the area be designed to meet certain earthquake-resistance standards. The Federal Housing Administration might deny loan insurance to such areas unless properties offered as security for insured-mortgage loans are built to earthquake-resistance specifications. The Department of Housing and Urban Development might deny all its financial support programs to earthquake-threatened areas, based on requirements that would include zoning and subdivision building codes that would acceptably reduce or eliminate the risks on a project-by-project basis. A similar approach has recently been taken to airport-related noise exposures,[14] where potential injuries are less grave than those from earthquakes.

One effect of such combined public- and private-sector constraints may be to limit further use and development in earthquake-threatened areas to those who can afford to purchase built-in earthquake resistance. In the absence of such constraints, speculative developers might exploit reduction in property values to entice low- and moderate-income families into the most vulnerable areas. With such constraints as stimuli, modifications of local land-use control regulations will probably receive public consideration.

If the prediction identifies an area of considerable size as threatened (e.g., a major segment of a metropolitan area or a rural sector encompassing perhaps several small communities), protective actions of this sort may not be feasible. The potential benefits to be derived from the constraints mentioned may be counterbalanced by the prospect that their imposition will result in the substantial exclusion of residential opportunities for low- and moderate-income families, and of small businesses. In order to retain the benefits from the constraints it will be necessary to make fine distinctions of vulnerability among neighborhoods. If technology can provide a means for identifying the types and degrees of vulnerability within potentially earthquake-threatened areas before a prediction is made, subsectors that are "safe" or feasibly "salvageable" may be sufficiently extensive that the land-use management and control and construction-regulatory processes could be employed to assure that normal developmental compositions and patterns will not be materially disrupted by a prediction or by a subsequent earthquake.

The capacity to capitalize on such potentials could be enhanced if the

---

[14]See *Noise Abatement and Control: Departmental Policy, Implementation Responsibility, and Standards,* Department of Housing and Urban Development, Circular No. 1390.2 (Washington, D.C.: U.S. Government Printing Office, August 1971), which provides for the following categories of exposure: acceptable; discretionary, normally acceptable; discretionary, normally unacceptable; and unacceptable.

traditional legal concept that building codes cannot be zoned[15] could be modified to a greater degree than it has been to date. The newly emerging and not yet fully developed concept of "transferrable development rights"[16] also holds promise of being particularly beneficial with respect to the types of "neighborhood-specific" land-use constraints discussed here. The reduction of earthquake hazards might be more readily achieved if zoning codes were written in terms of intended effects rather than in terms of the means to achieve these effects. For example, instead of specifying the use of a certain amount of diagonal bracing, such codes might require an ability to withstand the largest horizontal acceleration expected with 50 percent probability during the life of the building.

Any encouragement derived from the above suggestions must be tempered by the realization that, with respect to already existing structures and largely developed areas, there remains only a very limited potential for legal action. That potential is limited to zoning-code amortization provisions, to possible retroactive application of building codes, to housing-code coverages, and to emergency police powers of acquisition for community safety, all of which were mentioned earlier in this chapter. Beyond those processes there presently exists only the power of eminent domain, which can be coupled with urban-redevelopment programs, but which, with or without redevelopment, is too costly to be applicable comprehensively across large areas.

OTHER LEGAL ASPECTS OF EARTHQUAKE PREDICTION

Many other legal ramifications deserve examination in assessing an emerging capability for credible earthquake prediction. Only a few can be mentioned in the concluding section of this chapter.

Two questions regarding insurance are still unresolved: At the end of policy premium periods can an insuror withdraw coverage at will from an area identified by a prediction or threatened by an earthquake? How can adequate coverage be made available for risks thought to be clearly regional in nature? In the former case, some relevant experience has developed in the aftermath of the urban riots in the late 1960's; in the latter case, researchers have studied the problem with respect to flood insurance. Nevertheless, legislators and scholars have failed to develop any fully satisfactory solutions to these problems. Even the more narrow

---

[15]To satisfy constitutional equal protection requirements, such codes must be consistent in applicability throughout a jurisdiction.

[16]See, e.g., Jerome G. Rose, "A Proposal for the Separation and Marketability of Development Rights as a Technique to Preserve Open Space," *Real Estate Law Journal*, 2(3) (Winter 1974), 635.

issue of whether insurance protection should be limited to a specific type of event or should comprehensively cover all or a collection of disaster potentials remains unsettled.[17] The final answer to these questions will require not only specific legislation, but also the use of the regulatory process to achieve desired ends.

The question of the scope and extent of governmental emergency powers is complex and in large measure must be explored at federal, state, and local levels, with both statutory and constitutional considerations involved. The Disaster Relief Act of 1974 makes provision for federal disaster assistance in emergencies as well as major disasters. As defined in the Act, the term "emergency" means

any hurricane, tornado, storm, flood, high water, wind-driven water, tidal wave, tsunami, earthquake, volcanic eruption, landslide, mudslide, snowstorm, drought, fire, explosion, or other catastrophe in any part of the United States which requires Federal emergency assistance to supplement State and local efforts to save lives and protect property, public health and safety or to avert or lessen the threat of a disaster.[18]

A pertinent question is whether a credible earthquake prediction would be interpreted as an "emergency" under the provisions of this Act, thereby making predisaster assistance available to the communities and areas affected by the prediction. An additional pertinent question is whether, and to what degree, federal assistance might be available for pre-prediction earthquake-damage-mitigation efforts for sections of the nation considered to be particularly earthquake-prone.

Several legal aspects of earthquake prediction require further research before action can be taken. For example, studies comparing the adequacy of state and local disaster-related laws and assessing the usefulness of general programs of legislation that provide for the unique needs occasioned by specific disaster events cannot be effectively conducted until a comprehensive list of state and local disaster-related legislation is compiled.

A number of questions regarding earthquake prediction remain unexplored; among them are the following: What prediction events would or should justify official acts aimed at disaster mitigation? Under what circumstances, if any, might local decisions not to undertake hazard-reduction measures be overridden by higher authorities? Should regional institutions, either governmental or private, be established to enhance cooperation and coordination with respect to land-use management and other areas of responsibility? What are the limits of the author-

[17]See, e.g., Howard Kunreuther, "The Case for Comprehensive Disaster Insurance," *The Journal of Law and Economics,* XI (April 1968), 133.
[18]Public Law 93-288, 93rd Congress, S.3062, Disaster Relief Act of 1974, May 22, 1974.

ity and responsibility for one governmental entity to assist another? In a society as complex and as beset with problems as ours, we cannot afford to continue our present marginal attention to disaster potentials and consequences. Instead, we must examine all aspects of the questions raised above, for while these issues have many legal aspects, few can be dealt with solely on a legal basis.

SELECTED REFERENCES

Bosselman, Fred, and David Callies. *The Quiet Revolution in Land-Use Control,* Council on Environmental Quality. Washington, D.C.: U.S. Government Printing Office, 1971.

Brown, James M. "Beyond the Law and the Lab in Search of Public Safety Design Criteria," *Public Safety: A Growing Factor in Modern Design.* Washington, D.C.: National Academy of Sciences, 1970.

Dacy, Douglas C., and Howard Kunreuther. *The Economics of Natural Disaster: Implications for Federal Policy.* New York: The Free Press, 1969.

Green, Harold P. *The Law's Interface with Expanding Technology,* Occasional Paper No. 13, Program of Policy Studies in Science and Technology. Washington, D.C.: The George Washington University, August 1972.

Hagman, Donald G. *Urban Planning and Land Development Control Law.* St. Paul, Minnesota: West Publishing Co., 1971.

Kunreuther, Howard. "The Case for Comprehensive Disaster Insurance," *The Journal of Law and Economics,* 11 (April 1968), 133.

7 The Problem of Equity

Disasters strike different segments of the population unequally. A major purpose of disaster insurance and disaster relief has always been to spread the costs of disaster. With several months or years of advance warning prior to a major earthquake, we can take steps in advance of the disaster to protect those who otherwise would suffer most from the quake. In addition, the publication of an earthquake prediction will affect the wealth and welfare of the population unequally, and we should identify the probable gainers and losers so as to be able to judge which inequities are unacceptable. And, third, the very steps taken by government and public agencies to mitigate earthquake hazards will have costs that could easily fall unfairly on some segments of the community. These matters have been discussed throughout the report. But the problem of equity is so central to public policies that in spite of the repetition we should look at this area as a whole.

PROTECTING THE HARDEST HIT

The dangers of death and injury from an earthquake are greatest for people who live and work in substandard buildings that are structurally weak or vulnerable to fire. These buildings often are overcrowded and have inadequate access to emergency services. In sections of the country where building standards have been raised over the years to enhance earthquake resistance and fire resistance, the vulnerable structures are likely to be the older ones. A disproportionate number of the poor, the

The Problem of Equity

elderly, and members of minority groups reside in vulnerable housing.[1]

As awareness of earthquake hazards becomes more general, through the use of earthquake-risk maps and maps showing the locations of reservoirs and other sources of secondary danger, earthquake victims may include a disproportionate share of people who lack such awareness. Again, the less literate, the foreign-speaking, and those who have only recently moved from regions of less well-advertised earthquake risk are least likely to be aware of these dangers.

Among the people who survive an earthquake, the hardest hit will be (a) those who find their living and working quarters damaged and potentially vulnerable to aftershock but lack the resources to move to other quarters and (b) those who cannot get along when faced with temporary inconvenience. These groups include the aged and infirm, the impoverished, and people without nearby relatives or close friends on whom they can call for help.

UNCOORDINATED RESPONSES TO PREDICTION

Because earthquake predictions will specify the time and location of an expected quake, they will change the basis on which various groups in the community calculate their own interests. Traditional identification of fault locations and earthquake-prone regions affects land use and property values on a fairly stable and continuing basis. But a long-range prediction that localizes the immediate danger within the larger earthquake-prone area will instantly make some locations less desirable than others. For example, while there is one set of building codes for all of Los Angeles County and several faults that are mapped and known to investors, a prediction would identify a much more immediate danger in one section of the county. People who have commitments and investments in that section then stand to lose as a result of the prediction.

The prediction may affect people in the anticipated impact area by a sort of domino effect. For example, many people could be impelled to leave a threatened area not because of the earthquake warnings but because of increased unemployment brought on by the decision of key industrial firms to close their plants in order to avoid the prospect of

---

[1] Although specific data on the vulnerability of housing occupied by the poor, the elderly, and members of minority groups are not currently available, this statement appears to be a reasonable inference from existing U.S. Bureau of Census data on housing characteristics. For data on housing characteristics by income and ethnic characteristics, see U.S. Department of Commerce, Bureau of Census, *Census of Housing 1970: Metropolitan Housing Characteristics, U.S. and Regions,* Final Report HC (2)-1, 1972. For data on housing for the elderly, see U.S. Department of Commerce, Bureau of Census, Subject Report Number 2, *1970 Housing of Senior Citizens,* HC (7)-1, February 1973.

great property losses and uncertain liability for personal injury. While it may be consistent with good public policy to encourage some transfer of capital away from the threatened area in some instances, public intervention will be indispensable to ensure that the transfer is orderly and to ease the transition costs for those who otherwise will bear the brunt of the transfer.

The danger is that estimates of the total gain or loss to an area from an earthquake prediction could partially conceal balancing gains and losses to different segments of the community. For example, if people try to move away from the predicted center of quake activity but remain in the larger metropolitan area, the decline in property values near the center will be somewhat offset by rising property values elsewhere. Because of the movement of population, needed services to the community may be curtailed and relocated elsewhere. The offsetting gains elsewhere afford no comfort to the property owners and residents who are losing.

RECEIVING THE WARNING

Ability to take advantage of a warning depends first on people's receiving the warning and appreciating the implications of the warning for their interests. Constructive public policy should be designed to overcome some of the most serious differences among groups in these respects.

Whenever some people are privy to advance knowledge about events that may affect the value of property, goods, or services, they are placed in a position to gain, or at least to minimize their losses, at the expense of those who are not privy to the information.[2] For example, the property owner with advance information of the neighborhoods that will be affected by a soon-to-be publicized earthquake prediction may quickly sell his property before publication of the prediction affects the prices people are willing to pay. Because it is impossible to monopolize knowledge of the premonitory signs, because a period of time is required to interpret the signs and confirm a prediction, and because many people must be consulted before a confident prediction is made, the danger of information leaks is very great. Any considerations—legal, political, or other—that delay the release of significant information enhance the danger that a few insiders will benefit at the expense of outsiders.

Because inside information has value, organizations with heavy investments that might be affected by a prediction may decide to retain the

[2] Jack Hirshleifer, "The Private and Social Value of Information and the Reward for Inventive Activity," *American Economic Review,* 61 (September 1971), 561–574.

services of private seismologists and in other ways actively seek information in advance of public release. The problem here is similar to that confronted in the stock market. A study of procedures used, and of success and failure, in restricting unfair gain from inside information on the stock market should be helpful in approaching this problem. If current legislation does not suffice, it may be desirable to enact legislation that requires the immediate release of any information indicating that a potentially destructive earthquake is forthcoming or to provide for penalties and civil redress against persons and organizations who profit from such inside knowledge.

When warnings of immediate danger are issued, it is difficult to reach all the people in an affected area. Each medium of communication, such as radio or television, has its own special audience. The media can be supplemented by word of mouth in places where people typically gather together, e.g., in business establishments, schools, and in closely knit neighborhoods. But warnings are less likely to reach people in isolated residences and in apartment houses, where little intercommunication normally takes place. Here again, special thought must be given to the unattached, widowed, and otherwise isolated individuals, the elderly who do not circulate easily, and sight- and hearing-impaired individuals. Fortunately, if current thinking about earthquake precursors is correct, warnings of immediate danger should seldom occur except following earlier predictions or warnings for the areas in question. In anticipation of the time when seismologists develop the means for detecting the immediate onset of an earthquake, the issuance of a prediction should be the occasion for a careful study of the problems of communicating to those segments of the population that might otherwise receive only the final warning, and that belatedly.

When the warning concerns an event that is weeks to years in the future, the consequences of slight delays are not so serious. But unless a concerted effort is made to ensure that everyone has received the warning within a very few days, the prospect that uninformed populations will suffer disproportionate economic loss is substantial.

The problem of foreign-speaking residents is especially acute. A normal part of all disaster-preparedness activity should be to survey the foreign-speaking populace and prepare for issuance of warnings in several languages. For the most part, the foreign-speaking populace will be among the economically less advantaged, who are also disproportionately located in vulnerable housing and neighborhoods. But we should also give thought to foreign tourists in the United States. While long-range predictions are of little import to them, tourists are especially likely not to receive or understand warnings of immediate danger, and they are likely to be overlooked by agencies concerned with disseminating the warnings.

After a disaster has struck, the nature of damage and injury is generally evident to those most directly affected. But the risks to which people are subjected as a consequence of an earthquake *prediction* will not be equally evident until experience has been accumulated. People are not automatically in a position to recognize their interests in the face of complex economic, legal, and political maneuvering and unpredictable public response to the prediction. Before a group can take energetic action to promote its interests, it must first recognize them. Here the advantage plainly lies with those who are already represented by well-organized interest groups. The small property owner, the tenant, the employee in a nonunion establishment are among those especially likely not to recognize the potential threats to their interests until it is too late to take protective action. Programs to protect the consumer, such as those of the Food and Drug Administration and other federal and state agencies, constitute precedents for public agencies filling the gap, systematically monitoring the situation from the point of view of the interests of unorganized population segments, establishing systematic programs to keep these populations apprised of their interest, and recommending administrative and legislative actions to protect their interest.

ACTING ON THE WARNING

We have noted earlier that the greatest difficulty in many disaster-warning situations is overcoming *inaction.* People are slow to abandon their homes and familiar surroundings even in the face of serious threat. There is abundant reason to anticipate that many people in the vicinity of an expected quake will remain in the danger area and attempt to continue life as usual. The extended lead time in case of earthquake predictions adds a new dimension to the consequences of this normalization response. Inaction not only subjects the population to risk of injury and death, but it may also bring economic loss, unemployment, and inconvenience during the period between prediction and quake. The pattern of inaction in spite of these dangers may have both *sentimental* and *rational* bases. The attachment to home and familiar surroundings is the dominating sentimental basis. But there is also a rational basis for inaction because the predicted quake is not a certainty, because many people escape injury and serious loss even in the impact area, and because there is a good prospect of returning to normalcy after the quake and aftershock period are past. For the merchant who has a well-established business in the danger area, the costs and uncertainties of attempting to relocate his business may well seem to equal or exceed the risks of remaining.

But organizations whose interests in the affected area are minor in comparison with their interests outside the area may have sufficient reason to discontinue further investment in the area and to liquidate such investments as they can, even when there is only a moderately strong probability of a highly destructive earthquake. A nationwide merchandising establishment, for example, might prefer to absorb the costs of relocating methodically rather than to risk much greater loss in a quake. Here the domino effect will be important, as decisions by insurance companies and lending agencies increase the costs and risks of continuing in business, which in turn affect employment opportunities, and so on. If a substantial number of organizations and individuals whose major interests and commitments lie outside the affected area abandon the area that is in danger, those who are committed to the local area will personally or economically bear the costs disproportionately.

If large national establishments determine that their assets elsewhere are sufficient to warrant accepting the risks of continuing business in the threatened area, the problem just outlined will be minimized. But if they make the opposite judgment and positive and wide-ranging government action is not taken to maintain the local community, the locals—those committed to the affected area—will usually lose out in their conflict of interest with the cosmopolitans—those whose interests in the local area are secondary to their interests elsewhere.[3] In case of quite long-term predictions it is, of course, proper that government agencies consider the option of allowing extensive changes in the character of the affected area. But if this is done, it must be done with the explicit recognition that the interests of those who have most to lose must not be overlooked. This would suggest programs designed to help selectively those business and property owners who lack substantial interests outside of the area.

Since people who fail to act or who delay action stand to lose disproportionately, it is also important to take note of varying attitudes toward natural disaster among different population segments. It is well known that fatalistic views are especially prevalent among some of the less economically advantaged and among some ethnic and religious groups.[4] If

[3] See Robert K. Merton, "Patterns of Influence: Local and Cosmopolitan Influentials," *Social Theory and Social Structure* (New York: The Free Press, 1957), pp. 387–420.

[4] See Oscar Lewis, "The Culture of Poverty," *Scientific American*, 215 (October 1966), 3–9; Harry E. Moore, et al., *Before the Wind: A Study of the Response to Hurricane Carla*, Disaster Research Group, Disaster Research Study No. 19 (Washington, D.C.: National Academy of Sciences–National Research Council, 1963), especially pp. 124–125; and Lyle Saunders, *Cultural Difference and Medical Care* (New York: Russell Sage Foundation, 1954), pp. 128–133.

these groups are not to be victims of earthquake prediction, it will be necessary to study the distribution of fatalistic attitudes and seek ways to stimulate protective action among them.

ALTRUISM AND THE INVISIBLE CATASTROPHE

In most natural disasters the brutal impact on the victims is at least partially offset by the rise of an unusual spirit of altruism in the community.[5] For some people the *prediction* of an earthquake may be a catastrophe. But the damaging effects of the prediction are not tangible, visible, instantaneous, or dramatic. They are unlikely to be experienced as a near-miss by others in the community. The losses are more like an intensification of the normal hazards of life than the uniquely catastrophic evidence of a collapsed or burned building. Thus several of the supposed foundations for community altruism will be lacking in the case of losses that result from a prediction rather than from an actual quake. As an *invisible catastrophe,* a prediction that sets in motion a series of public and organizational responses that ultimately destroy the economic well-being or life style of a segment of the population is unlikely to evoke a sudden altruistic outpouring among the less affected.

The clear mandate of sympathy for the victims of natural catastrophe is further muted by the confusion over responsibility and blame. Although the prediction is based on natural events, the prediction is a human action, as are the political, economic, and mass responses to the prediction. The ambiguity of the situation is likely to inhibit much of the spontaneous outpouring of sympathy. The human agency invites preoccupation with the assignment of responsibility and blame. A preoccupation with blaming typically diverts energy from helping the victims as major attention is devoted to punishing the persons held to be at fault.[6]

It is important that public officials and media personnel understand that for these and other reasons they may not be able to count on the

---

[5]Allen H. Barton, *Communities in Disaster* (Garden City, N.Y.: Doubleday and Co., 1969), pp. 203–279; Russell R. Dynes, *Organized Behavior in Disaster* (Lexington, Mass.: D. C. Heath & Co., 1970), pp. 84–108.

[6]Harry E. Moore identified a "brickbat" stage in postdisaster response. See his *Tornadoes over Texas* (Austin: University of Texas Press, 1958), especially pp. 310–317. However, as Bucher has pointed out, blaming is not an inevitable by-product of disasters, nor is it usually focused on fortuitous or innocent scapegoat targets. Blame assessment is essentially a future-oriented response to disaster; agents who are blamed are not blamed for the disaster just past but for the disaster that may occur in the future unless appropriate remedial steps are taken. See Rue Bucher, "Blame and Hostility in Disasters," *American Journal of Sociology,* 62 (1957), 467–475.

The Problem of Equity 103

usual postcatastrophe surge of altruism to help those who are hurt by the prediction or to support programs aimed at mitigating invidious effects of prediction.

COORDINATED RESPONSES TO PREDICTION

If the uncoordinated efforts of individuals and organizations to protect themselves against loss from a predicted earthquake inadvertently undermine the well-being of some of the people, there is an equal danger that hazard-reduction programs instituted by responsible public agencies may sometimes hurt some of the people while helping others. A dilemma related to making buildings and other structures earthquake-resistant serves to illustrate the problem. One response to a long-term prediction might be to set stricter building standards in the indicated area and to insist on strengthening and fireproofing many existing structures. But if these expenses are borne by the property owner without offsetting reductions in insurance premiums, they substantially increase the cost of housing and business establishments. Every rise in the cost of housing forces more of the economically less well-endowed populations out of the market for conventional housing. Already a large share of low-income households have been forced into mobile homes, where they become especially vulnerable to tornadoes, hurricanes, and other severe storms.[7] Similarly, earthquake insurance augments the already high cost of housing. Any mandatory program of earthquake insurance might raise the premium threshold so that many family units could no longer afford adequate housing.

In addition to the unintended by-products of such well-intentioned programs, disproportionate loss and inconvenience may be sustained by the poor and politically less powerful when programs are selected as a result of the struggle among interest groups in the community. Land-use planning is an area of public policy that is heavily influenced by interest groups and highly responsive to political considerations in many American communities. The more economically and politically favored groups

[7]For 1974, the U.S. Bureau of Census reported that a total of 501,000 single-family, site-built homes were sold. For the 471,000 of these for which sales price reports were available, only 22,000—or 4.7 percent—sold for under $20,000. See U.S. Department of Commerce, Bureau of Census, *New One-Family Homes Sold and for Sale,* Construction Report C-25-75-2, February 1975. Mobile homes dominate the under-$20,000 shelter market. In 1974, it is estimated that 94 percent of all single-family dwellings selling for under $20,000 were mobile homes (estimates made by Elrick and Lavidge, Inc., Chicago, Illinois, for Mobile Homes Manufacturers Association, P.O. Box 201, Chantilly, Virginia 22021). Neither the Bureau of Census data nor the Elrick and Lavidge data include contractor- and owner-built homes or homes built for rent.

in the United States already gain the greatest advantages from the use of land. Under the guise of implementing land-use planning for hazard reduction following an earthquake prediction, existing inequities could be intensified.

Furthermore, whatever hazard-reduction programs are instituted, none is better than its implementation. Here again, the economically less-advantaged groups are less likely to benefit. For example, enforcement of building codes is notoriously lax in poor neighborhoods. Past experiences with postdisaster relief indicate that low-income groups may benefit little from public programs for mitigating earthquake hazards: Over 75 percent of the recipients of Small Business Administration disaster loans following the San Fernando earthquake of 1971 had incomes over $12,500.[8]

It is doubtful that any set of rules can be devised to ensure that the politically and economically weak are not the innocent victims of programs to lessen destruction and injury from a predicted earthquake. It may be essential to assign responsibility to some public agency to serve as watchdog in this regard. As plans are developed in response to a prediction, they should be monitored by the watchdog agency for inequitable features that might then be corrected before the plans are actually implemented. At the same time, it is important that plans to offset inequities not provide incentives for continuing exposure to possible hazards.

SELECTED REFERENCES

Dacy, Douglas C., and Howard Kunreuther. "Equity in Disaster Relief," *The Economics of Natural Disaster: Implications for Federal Policy.* New York: The Free Press, 1969. pp. 203–221.

Friedsam, Hiram J. "Older Persons in Disaster," *Man and Society in Disaster,* George W. Baker and Dwight W. Chapman (ed.). New York: Basic Books, 1962. pp. 151–184.

Moore, Harry E. *Tornadoes Over Texas: A Study of Waco and San Angelo in Disaster.* Austin: University of Texas Press, 1958. pp. 88–152.

---

[8]See Howard Kunreuther, *Recovery from Natural Disasters* (Washington, D.C.: American Enterprise Institute for Public Policy Research, 1973), p. 32.

8 Political Implications of Earthquake Prediction

Public officials will ultimately have to resolve the many uncertainties of earthquake prediction to the best of their abilities and exercise leadership in dealing with them. The effectiveness of their programs will depend largely on the initiative and competence of agency personnel within the government. In this chapter we shall try to identify the difficulties that officials will confront when a prediction is made, the political circumstances that may influence their actions, and the possibilities of their winning support for constructive programs. In doing so we are limited to speculating on the basis of prior experience in constructive programs. We shall also consider how constructive government action can be facilitated in connection with earthquake predictions.

EARTHQUAKE PREDICTION AS A POLITICAL ISSUE

Mitigation of earthquake hazards has been a lively political issue immediately after damaging quakes, and significant legislation has sometimes been enacted then. For example, the California legislature enacted the Field and Riley acts dealing with school buildings and other construction, respectively, in the aftermath of the 1933 Long Beach earthquake. Similarly, several legislative enactments resulted from the 1971 San Fernando quake. Interest flags soon after the crisis, however. Little has been done in the four decades since the Long Beach quake to bring older structures up to standard. On the other hand, building-code and land-use ordinances based on safety from seismic disturbances have been reasonably well enforced in new construction. There has been little disposition to repeal such legislation, and even so controversial a local regulation as the city-planning-based restrictions on the height of buildings in the City of Los Angeles survived until 1957. Significant advances in earthquake-hazard reduction can be achieved if well-conceived legislation and administrative regulations are introduced in the favorable political climate immediately after an earthquake disaster and if authority for implementation is vested in strong and independent government agencies.

How will a prediction, as contrasted with an actual quake, affect the political process? Response to the first such prediction will surely be quite different from responses to later predictions. A series of predictions for different earthquakes extending over several decades may be required to resolve legal uncertainties and establish firm political precedents.

If the announced prediction has been given credence in the scientific community, and if there is only a short interval of days or weeks before the anticipated event, the effect on the political process may be much like that of a real earthquake. There will be insistent demands that political differences be laid aside. Many in the threatened area will expect officials to call for sacrifices and will respond most readily to the leadership of those who do. There is a good possibility that media coverage will be conducive to a climate of opinion in the state, and perhaps in the nation, favorable to the provision of assistance to threatened communities. If well-conceived pre-prediction plans are already on hand at local, state, and national levels, capable local and state leaders may win support for what would otherwise be quite extraordinary programs. Without pre-prediction planning, however, the frustrated public demand for immediate and comprehensive action may well contribute to community conflict and counterproductive government action.

If the predicted lead time is in months or years and the probability of error is substantial, the earthquake prediction will be a less compelling political issue. A stricter application of existing building standards; intensified inspection of schools, hospitals, and lifelines; strengthening of emergency services; and other familiar measures should win considerable support. But any initial consensus is likely to dissipate soon, and there will be a growing temptation for public officials to try to shift the focus of political discourse to other issues or other levels of government. First, the agencies to which officials would most naturally turn are offices of emergency services, state and local police and sheriff's forces, and private agencies such as the Red Cross or Salvation Army. But these agencies are organized primarily for the prompt mobilization of rescue, relief, and other emergency services. These are not the principal tasks that need to be undertaken during the early period of a long-term prediction. The most relevant agencies are those concerned with planning for land use, economic development, building construction, and public welfare. There could well be struggles for control within the government between planning and emergency agencies.

Second, the awareness of divergent interests will soon come to the fore. Some powerful groups will undoubtedly see threats to their economic interests in the recognition and response to the prediction. If the poor, minorities, and the aged find themselves in the old and substandard housing most vulnerable to earthquake hazard, political discourse may soon become polarized along the traditional lines that divide the haves from the have-nots. And as the proponents of ongoing programs unrelated to earthquakes become threatened by the prospect that substantial resources could be diverted from their projects, conflict will develop with agency personnel and private firms that benefit from the diversion.

Third, public officials are often expected to have solved in advance the problems associated with foreseeable crises such as earthquakes. Consequently, the prediction may be grasped as a timely issue by the political opposition, who criticize the incumbents' lack of foresight and expose weak enforcement of building codes and disregard of fault locations in the placement of buildings.

Finally, the element of uncertainty in all earthquake predictions will plague public officials at every step, and this uncertainty is likely to reinforce the political predisposition to shift the focus to other issues or to other levels of government.

PREDICTIONS, WARNINGS, AND THE POLITICAL PROCESS

In many instances, predictions issued by seers and pseudoscientists can be quickly refuted by referral to established scientific representatives and their consequence in the political process minimized. But predictions bearing the stamp of scientific authenticity subject public officials to immediate demands for clarification and action. Since the mass communication media usually vigorously relay such demands, the stage can be quickly set for a confrontation between public officials who are slow to respond and the mass media.

Again the situation is politically quite different, depending upon whether the lead time is estimated as a few hours or days or several months or years. With a short-term prediction that is authenticated in the scientific community, a moderate degree of uncertainty over the prediction should not be a politically telling deterrent to issuing the warning. Nevertheless, circumstances may contribute to reluctance and delay.

First, threatened areas will usually overlap political boundaries, and prompt agreement among civil units may not be attained easily.[1] Second, public officials often have an understandable but unjustified fear of public panic, as discussed in Chapter 4. And third, public officials often fear that people will ignore the next warning if the first prediction does not come true. This fear, too, may be greater than experience warrants.

When the prediction carries a longer lead time, delay in issuing a warning from lack of urgency will allow interests opposed to issuing any warning to be heard. Moreover, an extended time window for occurrence is especially threatening. Official warnings, even without further implementation, may cause people to fear freeways, bridges, and tunnels and to eschew travel to the central city where tall buildings abound; they may have an adverse effect on the tourist industry and may discourage new building and the establishment of new business enterprises in the threatened area. A representative of the business community recently estimated that such disruptions, if continued for several months, might cost San Francisco as much as three billion dollars. Accordingly, he recommended that "predictions should be considered only when the system has been found perfect." The mayor of another large metropolis declared, "the reliability of earthquake forecasting needs to be established beyond a reasonable doubt before any attempt is made to institute a public alert system." A typical view is expressed by a director of California's Office of Emergency Planning: "Until accuracy is fully established, all earthquake predictions should be released as items of information and not as warnings."[2]

As we noted in Chapter 2, predictions will almost surely be forthcoming, and almost as surely during the foreseeable future, they will have to be stated in terms of probability rather than certainty. Public officials will sometimes be tempted to join in attacks on scientists and their predictions, to seek out dissenting scientists who will lend authenticity to the challenge, or at least to caution a wait-and-see attitude until the scientific community is more confident. Another kind of response would shift responsibility to the state and federal levels.

Another public official concludes, probably correctly: "After an initial

---

[1]Virtually all metropolitan areas have a multiplicity of overlapping political jurisdictions. For instance, in Los Angeles County there are over 340 special districts performing local government functions. Approximately half of these districts are governed by the county Board of Supervisors, but the remainder are controlled by separate elected boards of directors. In addition, there are 77 cities within Los Angeles County.

[2]These statements are derived from testimony given to the Joint Committee on Seismic Safety of the California legislature, chaired by Senator Alfred E. Alquist, December 13, 1974, and from letters received by the Panel on the Public Policy Implications of Earthquake Prediction from mayors and other officials from the State of California.

phase of uneasy discussion, most people will subscribe to the logic that warnings must be issued; there is no choice. Political and community pressure would overwhelm those who may at first be reluctant about release of a warning." Withholding the warning could subject an official to the charge of being willing to trade lives for dollars. The consequence of delay in issuing the warning will likely be a residue of bitterness and distrust and a weakening of initial support for difficult actions.

The stress surrounding issuance of warnings will undoubtedly lead to efforts to control *who* may issue predictions and to standardize the grounds on which they are made.[3] In the short run these pressures could lead to excessive caution or to actions based on political considerations rather than scientific judgment. Early collaboration among the U.S. Geological Survey, the Federal Disaster Assistance Administration, and agencies in key states to develop guidelines and a program for educating the public to the realities of earthquakes and predictions are urgently needed to help forestall dangerous developments and also to strengthen the hands of public officials in issuing warnings promptly. The tasks of both elected and appointed local officials will be eased by state and federal participation and guidelines.

PUBLIC TASKS AND GRASS-ROOTS SUPPORT

Tasks confronting public officials after a warning has been issued are of three kinds. The most easily understood and justified and the least controversial politically are tasks having to do with *preparation for postdisaster emergency response and recovery*. Government agencies such as police, fire departments, and emergency health-care units will find the climate propitious for enlarging and improving their operational base by adding such resources as surveillance helicopters, ambulances, emergency communication systems, improved firefighting equipment, and personnel.[4]

The objective of mobilizing public support for constructive action can be felicitously combined with useful steps in disaster preparedness by organizing public participation in this phase of the response. Training in emergency skills such as first aid could be organized on a massive scale

---

[3]It is possible that in the near future some states—and California would seem a likely candidate—may require some type of state license for those making predictions. Holders of the license might have to meet certain qualifications and become subject to peer-review procedures. This kind of licensing is an extension of the current practice, which sees many types of professions and occupations under state licensing control.

[4]The way in which the importance of an agency's function contributes to changes within an agency, including expansion of staff, is discussed extensively in Anthony Downs, *Inside Bureaucracy* (Boston: Little, Brown, 1967).

in the months just before the predicted event. Opportunities for citizen participation on a smaller scale could be usefully scheduled throughout a long period of advance warning. Active involvement by a wide spectrum of citizens in preparing for the crisis should foster support for the more difficult and costly steps that must also be taken.

The two remaining sets of tasks, though even more significant in their contribution to reducing loss of life and property, are politically more hazardous for public officials. Although the public will readily appreciate the need for *devising and implementing hazard-reduction plans,* such as condemnation and demolition of unsafe structures and restriction of movement in danger areas, opposition is sure to develop. The third set of tasks, *coping with potentially counterproductive responses to the prediction,* such as unemployment resulting from withdrawal of mortgage money for construction, may come as a surprise to most of the public. Unfamiliarity with the problem and a tendency to see it as man-made rather than naturally induced could create a difficult climate for officials attempting to control adverse developments resulting from actions taken by industrial, business, and other groups and agencies both within and outside the local jurisdiction.

If lead times of weeks or a few months are available, citizen participation can be used, both to help implement hazard-reduction measures and to mobilize community support. Existing voluntary groups in the community can be utilized to help in posting safe and unsafe facilities, to devise community plans for the actions to be taken as the time of the predicted quake approaches, to inform public officials about individuals who may suffer because of hazard-reduction measures, and to encourage community cooperation.

The problems of hazard reduction and coping with counterproductive developments from earthquake prediction will be new and relatively unfamiliar to most public officials, though not unlike problems they normally confront in other connections. Local occurrences during anyone's lifetime will be too few to establish an experience-based set of popularly accepted guidelines to which the official can refer to assure public support. Efforts to anticipate and forestall counterproductive developments will attract little support, yet citizens may be quick to blame the local official if the rates of business and employment activity decline and if earthquake insurance policies are cancelled. Hence it will be important for officials to seek guidance from a group of respected technical advisers and to filter their proposed policies and decisions through a larger citizens' group. If these are acting rather than delaying bodies, they should help transfer the difficult decisions out of the realm of political controversy and make some contribution to public confidence.

RESOURCES AND THE FEDERAL GOVERNMENT

Despite some concerns about local autonomy, the limited resources of local and even state governments practically guarantee an early decision to call for federal aid. The key problems of dealing with unsafe structures and bolstering a threatened local economy are sure to be costly. A local or state bond issue to raise large sums to rebuild unsafe structures would encounter widespread opposition from taxpayers' associations, from groups whose lives and businesses would be disrupted in the interim (residents, owners, local merchants), and from owners who have already paid their own money to finance quake-resistant construction.

Federal involvement will also be important in other respects. The infrequency of serious quakes prevents accumulation of experience in local communities and requires that officials look to state and federal agencies for technical guidance. Federal involvement may serve the local official as a buffer against the uncertain and volatile pattern of support for earthquake-reduction programs in the community. And, as we have discussed in Chapter 5, once a prediction has been issued—with or without a formal warning—officers of nationwide or multinational financial and business establishments may hold the fate of the community's economy in their hands. With little that can be done locally or even at the state level to control or compensate for such decisions, the community's only hope will appear to lie in federal action.

Can threatened communities expect timely and substantial assistance from the federal government? Where there are potentially vulnerable military installations and other large unrecoverable investments by the federal government, the interested federal agencies could contribute to a stabilization of the affected economy by increasing their monetary investments in the area.

The key to many kinds of federal assistance seems to lie in some extrapolation from existing legislation under which a community is declared a disaster area and thereby made eligible for low-cost building loans and many other services.[5] But the tendency to view earthquakes as regional problems can impede negotiation of a massive supportive federal response. The infrequency of serious quakes prevents the routine inclusion of funds to aid earthquake-threatened communities in the annual budget of any federal agency. Each instance will therefore mean a fresh appeal to Congress. The absence of a visible catastrophe and the element of uncertainty surrounding the prediction may impair any nationwide

---

[5]Public Law 93-288, the Disaster Relief Act of 1974, provides the current basis for federal assistance in peacetime disasters.

outpouring of sympathy. The principle of compensating people for the loss of valuable property before it has actually been destroyed by an "act of nature" will be difficult to promote. Viewed as a local issue, the earthquake threat might go the way of airport noise abatement, which has been dealt with through action in the courts rather than vigorous legislative initiative. However, the chance of attracting a few vigorous legislative spokesmen is better because the earthquake threat affects entire constituencies as well as neighborhoods. The prospects for some log-rolling success are reasonably favorable, with support for relief in connection with annual hurricane, tornado, and flood threats in less earthquake-prone states the possible trade-off.

The federal approach to new problems is typically characterized by *incrementalism*, i.e., extending and adapting old programs to new situations rather than devising wholly new approaches.[6] Here lie the best prospects for prompt federal involvement. A proposal to expand currently subsidized flood or wind insurance programs to include earthquakes would gain a hearing, even though the utility of this approach is in question. The precedent of federally guaranteed or underwritten loans for construction and purchase of homes and business buildings might be used to compensate for the reluctance of private lending institutions to invest where high risk has been identified. Urban redevelopment affords another precedent that might be adapted to suit the situation. Extended periods of eligibility for unemployment compensation under social security have been used in dealing with other crises.

POPULATION EVACUATION AND RELOCATION

Evacuation is a familiar approach to such local threats as flood, hurricane, explosion, and tsunami. Much energy may be diverted into drawing up evacuation plans and debating the merits of this approach. But extensive evacuation will usually be politically unacceptable. Public officials and business leaders will fear that if people are encouraged to evacuate for an extended period, many will move away permanently, undermining the community and its economy. Even a cursory study of what is involved in establishing "relocation centers" or "refugee camps" will soon demonstrate the magnitude of the task of massive community evacuation.

Vacating unsafe structures and evacuating small numbers of people

[6]Incrementalism has been discussed throughout the literature of political science. See, for example, Theodore J. Lowi, *End of Liberalism* (New York: Norton, 1969); David Braybrooke and Charles Lindblom, *A Strategy of Decision* (New York: Free Press, 1963); Aaron Wildavsky, *The Politics of the Budgetary Process* (Boston: Little, Brown, 1964).

Political Implications of Earthquake Prediction

from previously identified unsafe localities merit serious study, however. But here the issue of how far the authorities should go in ordering and enforcing evacuation becomes political. Experience with tsunamis and other threats indicates an uncertain response to voluntary evacuation plans. When danger is imminent and obvious, as it was in the area below the Lower San Fernando Dam following the San Fernando earthquake of 1971, general compliance with an order for evacuation can often be achieved with little difficulty. But with a long lead time, no visible threat, an acknowledged amount of uncertainty over the prediction and the quake's effects, and the possibility that the evacuation may last for weeks or months, evacuation plans will certainly become the target for political controversy. In such a climate of opinion the police would often be reluctant to enforce compliance even if they had the authority. The evacuation question may raise the issue of the government's right to compel people to protect themselves.

With a long-term prediction, the more extreme course of relocating or dispersing whole communities will be suggested, especially by people located outside the targeted areas. When human sentiment and political realities are disregarded, it can sometimes be shown that the dollar cost of relocating the community will be less than the estimated dollar loss from the quake and prediction in combination. A lead time of several years can provide the suitable occasion for relocating or dismantling a community that should not originally have been built at a place of recurrent danger. The argument that people *can* relocate, with the help of low-cost loans and liberal tax concessions, might be used in opposition to outright state and federal grants to maintain the community. But precedent is clear: Even relocating a small community for a permanent installation such as a dam is politically difficult.[7] Strong appeals to sentiment and tradition in the community will strike a responsive political chord. The ultimate policy decision at all levels, perhaps after months or years of indecision, will almost certainly be to preserve the threatened communities as they now exist rather than to relocate.

UNSAFE STRUCTURES AND THE UNCERTAIN GOOD

As noted in Chapter 3, most earthquake deaths occur when buildings or parts of buildings collapse or fall on people. If extensive evacuation or relocation is not feasible, the most important problem facing officials is what to do about unsafe structures. Much new construction will have to

---

[7] A useful example of this problem comes from the efforts to construct the Dos Rios Dam in Northern California. For one account of this episode, see L. Cannon, *Ronnie and Jesse: A Political Odyssey* (Garden City, N.Y.: Doubleday, 1969).

be suspended several months before the danger period commences, so there will be no structurally incomplete buildings to collapse in the quake. Existing unsafe structures must be reinforced, vacated, cordoned off, or demolished. But conflict will occur over the taking of private property and the dispossession of people. Officials must formulate their plans with several potent political considerations in mind.

First, there should be a sense of active preparation for the quake rather than passive waiting. Both economically and politically the suspension of activity will be fatal. If, for example, unsafe structures are simply abandoned, they will quickly become a blight on the community, an open invitation to squatters, and a visible sign that the community is waiting for disaster. When these steps are legally and economically feasible, demolition of dangerous structures—or, given sufficient lead time, an active rebuilding program—is to be preferred.

Second, the economically depressing effect of limiting construction and interrupting business activity during demolition and rebuilding must be anticipated and, when substantial, made a central consideration in planning the response. When new construction is discontinued, intensified work on structures that can be satisfactorily upgraded, and last-minute demolition of buildings that need not be replaced at once, could be scheduled to maintain the construction industry. Tourism might even increase before the immediate danger period, though tourists may be resented by local residents. Many of the unsafe structures may be clustered in the central business district. Demolition of a contiguous cluster of buildings here could threaten the economic base of the district by the sizable interruption of business activity, even though some owners of old buildings might welcome this way of freeing their investments in the absence of a market for their property.

Third, the many unanticipated costs of earthquake preparation can quickly become political irritants as efforts are made to pass them on to property owners and others. For example, if unsafe structures have not been previously identified, a fee charged each owner to cover inspection costs, or an item added to the property tax, may especially provoke resentment. This is one of many problems that can be minimized only if a long-term and continuous earthquake mitigation program has been in effect, including the identification of safe and unsafe structures, before the prediction is made.

Fourth, public officials must contend with a lack of clear and stable understanding of self-interest among many groups. This is likely to be true of the poor and minority groups, who often live and work in unsafe buildings. At first blush it seems obvious that their personal safety should be the uppermost concern for inhabitants of substandard housing, leading them to support stricter building-code enforcement and demolition of buildings coupled with rebuilding or relocation to safe housing. But the conviction is widespread that codes have more to do with protecting the building industry than with the safety of occupants, and that code enforcement is a sure prelude to increased rents. Redevelopment is often viewed as a device for displacing the poor to make room for a wealthier or socially more acceptable class of tenants. Overtones of racial oppression often develop. In addition, these groups may experience conflict between a definition based on their safety and economic self-interest and a definition based on psychological and social ties to their community and their history.[8]

If public leaders are not to have necessary programs undermined by opposition from these groups and their supporters in the community at large, carefully developed plans for interim and permanent rehousing of endangered populations must be presented at the same time that demolition is proposed. It is not politically feasible, even if it were otherwise acceptable, to let low-income and minority groups who occupy substandard housing bear the full costs of reconstruction.[9]

Fifth, officials will encounter conflicting demands to restore neighborhoods as they were before demolition and to rebuild according to an updated community-wide plan. Certainly the community's best interests will be served by seizing the opportunity for a fresh planning effort. Replacing old buildings with new ones according to an obsolete city design will only perpetuate existing problems for many more years. But many vested interests and a sense of urgency will speak for restoring the city as it was.[10]

With this, as with many problems facing officials, by the time a prediction is issued it is already too late for optimal planning, though much could still be accomplished. If buildings nearing the end of their useful life are regularly identified as part of a continuing community planning program, and plans have been previously made to take advantage of

---

[8]For discussion of the politics of housing in urban, low-income communities, see Michael Lipsky, *Protest in City Politics* (Chicago: Rand McNally, 1969); and Jewel Bellush and Murray Hausknecht, *Urban Renewal* (Garden City, N.Y.: Anchor Books, 1967).

[9]See Lipsky, *op. cit.*, and Bellush and Hausknecht, *op. cit.* The federal highway program now requires that those displaced by construction be relocated prior to actual construction.

[10]The disaster research literature shows an overwhelming tendency to rebuild and restore cities in the same ecological pattern as existed before a disaster. Even where cities have been virtually destroyed, as in the World War II bombing of Western Europe, they have usually been rebuilt on the same site and in the same general ecological pattern as before the war. See, for example, L. Grebler, "Continuity in the Re-building of Bombed Cities in Western Europe," *American Journal of Sociology* (March 1956), 463–469.

their eventual demolition, there will already be a strong foundation on which to promote planned rather than haphazard rebuilding.

COORDINATION AND CONTINUITY

We have already observed that an earthquake is no respecter of civil boundaries, so effective response will depend upon coordinated decisions and actions in several jurisdictions. With politically volatile issues such as those surrounding condemnation, demolition, and rebuilding of unsafe structures and rezoning, the uncertain support within each jurisdiction may prevent dependable agreements between jurisdictions. Inaction is often easier to defend in a court of law than mistaken action, so public officials may be tempted to let matters drift. Here the courageous action in one jurisdiction can force the hands of officials in neighboring jurisdictions, and cooperative action may be imposed as a condition for the receipt of federal assistance.

Coordination and continuity will be threatened by shifting public concerns during the course of a long-term prediction and by changes of office holders. The longer the prediction lead time, the more continuity of policy and program will depend upon vesting responsibilities for the programs in governmental agencies that have broad and long-range community planning functions (e.g., planning, engineering, and building departments). Continuity can also be served by bringing such interjurisdictional organizations as the Southern California Association of Governments, the Association of Bay Area Governments, The League of California Cities, and regional planning agencies into the planning process.

COMMUNITIES WITH LOW EARTHQUAKE AWARENESS

Some concluding comments are needed concerning regions such as parts of the eastern seaboard and the Mississippi Valley where the risk of a serious earthquake appears to be substantial, but popular and governmental awareness of the risk is low. While public pressure would almost certainly force reluctant local officials in California and Alaska into some kind of action, officials in other areas will have greater freedom to de-emphasize a warning and take no significant action. The problems of devising a constructive program in communities and areas with low earthquake awareness will be greater than in high-awareness areas, even apart from the deficiency in public awareness and support. Very little progress toward imposing standards for earthquake-resistant construction has been made in these areas. Hence demolition and rebuilding of unsafe structures would call for unacceptably high levels of expenditure and serious disruption of normal business and social life. Furthermore, earthquakes in these regions have in the past been less localized in relation to well-identified faults than western quakes have, so selective evacuation to nearby safe locations may be less feasible.

While it is difficult at present to formulate a constructive response for these areas, and while gaining substantial political support for a plan may be a formidable task, the possible saving of lives on the basis of a prediction should be much greater than in the western states. Much of the California population would be relatively safe during a major quake because they live and work in earthquake-resistant structures. But few structures in the East and Midwest have been designed to be quake-resistant. If it were practicable to get people safely away from most buildings, an earthquake prediction in these sections of the United States could forestall a disaster that might otherwise equal or exceed the toll of 8,000 lives lost in the Managua, Nicaragua, quake of 1972.

Earthquake prediction is less imminent in these areas than it is in the western states, so our discussion deals with a more remote and uncertain future. However, the uncertain prospect of prediction does not lessen the prospect of disastrous earthquakes outside of Alaska, Hawaii, and other western states—a prospect that deserves more attention and planning than it has received.

SELECTED REFERENCES

Bellush, Jewel, and Murray Hausknecht. *Urban Renewal.* Garden City, N.Y.: Anchor Books, 1967.

Braybrooke, David, and Charles Lindblom. *A Strategy of Decision.* New York: Free Press, 1963.

Cannon, L. *Ronnie and Jesse: A Political Odyssey.* Garden City, N.Y.: Doubleday, 1969.

Cotter, Cornelius P. *Jet Tanker Crash.* Lawrence, Kansas: The University Press of Kansas, 1968.

Joint Committee on Seismic Safety of the California State Legislature. *Meeting the Earthquake Challenge: Final Report to the Legislature, State of California.* Sacramento: Joint Committee on Seismic Safety, January 1974.

Lipsky, Michael. *Protest in City Politics.* Chicago: Rand McNally, 1969.

Rosow, Irving. "Public Authorities in Two Tornadoes." Unpublished report, Committee on Disaster Studies. Washington, D.C.: National Academy of Sciences–National Research Council, 1954.

Scott, Stanley (ed.). *In the Interest of Earthquake Safety: Findings and Conclusions by Members of the Task Force on Earthquake Hazard Reduction; Office of Science and Technology, Executive Office of the President.* Berkeley, Calif.: Institute of Government Studies, University of California, 1971.

9 Some Potentially Constructive Responses to Earthquake Warning

In Chapter 4 we examined the circumstances that might affect the issuance of predictions and warnings of earthquakes. In Chapter 3 we divided the strategy for responding to a warning into three parts, as follows: implementing a hazard-reduction program to minimize the loss of life and property and community disruption when the quake occurs; readying emergency services to deal with the situation after the quake has occurred; and controlling and offsetting potentially counterproductive consequences of the prediction. In addition we called attention to the need for pre-prediction planning for each set of tasks. In subsequent chapters we reviewed the potential impact of economic, legal, equity, and political considerations on the development and implementation of strategies for responding to warnings. In this chapter we shall attempt to bring together in summary form the many possible elements that make up a comprehensive response strategy.

As we review Chapters 5 through 8, three main conclusions stand out. First, both the consequences of most specific measures and the practical possibilities for putting them into effect are quite uncertain at the present time. Much will depend upon (a) private-sector decisions by national business leaders; (b) whether legislation and laws facilitate or impede constructive response; and (c) the stability of the political base for local public officials. Hence, any effort to follow a rigidly prescribed plan for responding to earthquake warning will surely lead the community into a deepening morass of problems. The more effective approach will be to work from a catalog of specific measures, applied selectively and flexibly

Some Potentially Constructive Responses to Earthquake Warning 119

according to the local situation, with careful monitoring for effectiveness and for changing conditions.

The second main conclusion is that the prospects for saving lives on the basis of an earthquake prediction are much clearer at this time than the prospects for substantial reduction in property loss. In years to come, as experience enables us to establish legal precedents and legislation to facilitate prompt and effective action, and as uncertainties of economic response are resolved, the savings of property and income in comparison with the costs of an unpredicted quake may be substantial. But for the first prediction of a potentially destructive earthquake it is difficult to estimate the ratio of savings to costs. By contrast, we know that lives can be saved if we make sure that people are located at safe distances from vulnerable buildings and other structures and are also protected against such derivative dangers as fire when the quake occurs. We know, too, that the saving in lives may in some instances number in the thousands.

It is essential that leaders in both public and private sectors keep these two conclusions in mind as they prepare to deal with specific earthquake predictions and warnings. Otherwise, it will be easy to slip into rigid formats. And it will be easy to lose sight of the great potential for saving lives while preoccupied with economic costs incurred as a result of a prediction.

The third main conclusion is that the feasibility of developing an effective response to earthquake warning at reasonable expense is enhanced when the community has had a long-term program of earthquake preparedness. The more people live, work, study, and play in earthquake-resistant structures, and the more consistently community planners and other public and private officials take account of earthquake danger, the more manageable will be the tasks confronting leaders in the public and private sectors when a quake is predicted. The focus of this entire report is on the steps that can be taken in the event of a prediction. But as we examine these measures, we are constantly reminded that a constructive program for utilizing earthquake prediction builds on and supplements a long-term program of planning for earthquakes and cannot be substituted for continuing efforts to identify and build defenses against earthquake hazard.

In this chapter we shall offer more detail for the brief outline of strategy presented in Chapter 3. Because "the opportunity to mount a carefully considered program of hazard reduction before the quake occurs is the unique and potentially most important contribution of earthquake prediction to saving lives and property and averting community disruption" (Chapter 3, p. 42), we shall deal with hazard reduction first and in greatest detail. The measures that might be employed with good effect will differ according to the period of advance warning. Hence, we shall examine the possibilities for action separately by length of advance warning.

Which of these measures should and should not be employed must be determined on the basis of the unique and changing circumstances in the threatened community, taking into account some reasonable estimates of (a) the ratio of anticipated benefits to economic costs, (b) the ratio of anticipated benefits to social costs, (c) the probability of occurrence of the earthquake as predicted, (d) the length of time prior to the predicted date of the quake, and (e) the duration of the time window within which the quake is predicted to occur.

LAND-USE PLANNING AND MANAGEMENT

The opportunities presented by the prospect of a long period of advance warning are best realized through land-use planning and management and through structural design and maintenance. The objective of land-use planning is always to locate structures and activities according to a rational plan rather than haphazardly. It is implemented through such devices as zoning ordinances, grading codes, microrisk mapping, and taxation policies. As an approach to the reduction of earthquake hazards, land-use management means siting the most vulnerable facilities and the greatest concentrations of people away from the places where the potential danger is greatest.

Land-use planning in the United States is mostly a local community effort, with occasional state involvement, and little direct federal participation, although there are some signs of changes in the direction of increased federal responsibility. The federal government can exercise considerable influence, however, by making acceptable land-use planning procedures a condition for awarding grants and matching funds to local communities. The implementation of planning for land use is extensively limited by private ownership. Planning activities must combine and compromise a variety of goals and interests, of which reducing earthquake hazard is only one. Hence, the reduction of earthquake hazards through land-use planning and management requires extended negotiation and cooperation to harmonize public safety considerations with other concerns for community welfare and private interest.

When informed planning and substantial execution of plans takes place over an extended period of time, land-use planning and management can be among the most effective measures for saving lives and property and minimizing disruption in case of an earthquake. Its use becomes even more important as population density increases.

The effectiveness of land-use planning depends upon being able to pinpoint specific zones of relative safety and danger. The earthquake prediction adds significant new information concerning places of greatest risk, which can then be the basis for revised planning when the period of advance warning is long enough. For greatest effectiveness, such revised planning will be selectively applied to critical facilities that could generate secondary threats in case of an earthquake (e.g., zoos, some kinds of storage depots, nuclear power plants), to facilities necessary for emergency response (e.g., hospitals, communication centers, fire departments), and to structures in which large numbers of people assemble (e.g., schools).

Because land-use planning requires extended periods of time, it cannot be suddenly implemented when the length of warning is only a matter of weeks or months. Being of intense concern to many interest groups, land-use planning is highly responsive to political pressures and subject to intense resistance to change and incredibly complex litigation. If previous experience in trying to develop better land use with respect to floods and flood plains is any indicator, it will not be easily or quickly implemented.

Nevertheless, the great potential for saving lives and property and the possibility of using the warning to strengthen long-term planning while preparing for the quake merit very serious attention to land-use planning and management.

STEPS THAT MIGHT BE TAKEN WITH ONE OR SEVERAL YEARS OF ADVANCE WARNING

1. A detailed map of earthquake hazard in the threatened area should be prepared and published, modifying existing quake-risk maps to take account of the predicted quake location and magnitude. The map should be revised from time to time as the prediction is modified or made more precise.

2. A land-use survey of the threatened area should be conducted, relating land use to risk, so as to identify the facilities that pose the greatest danger to life and property.

3. Existing land-use plans should be promptly modified to reflect the new pattern of risk, and zoning ordinances should be amended appropriately. Private-sector interests must be well represented in this and other efforts involving land use if they are to be effective.

4. Special attention should be devoted to lifeline elements in high-risk locations. Responsible officials in the private and public sectors should weigh the relative merits of dealing with identified hazards by removing,

replacing, or strengthening such critical facilities and by developing other plans to offset the danger.

5. Public officials should explore the possibilities for using taxation policies and other mechanisms at their disposal to encourage the modified use or selective removal of critical structures in very high-risk locations.

6. Careful study should be initiated to determine the most appropriate land-use patterns to apply to the impacted areas following the occurrence of the predicted earthquake.

7. Community officials, in consultation with seismologists and structural engineers, should establish a schedule of deadlines for the initiation of specified kinds of new construction according to areas of risk and deadlines for requiring unfinished structures to conform to acceptable safety standards, so as to minimize the hazard from the collapse of unfinished structures.

STEPS THAT MIGHT BE TAKEN WITH LESS THAN ONE YEAR OF ADVANCE WARNING

1. Existing land-use information or a quick survey might be used as a basis for identifying relatively dangerous or safe locations and for suspending new construction permits where the presence of an unfinished building might be hazardous.

2. To the extent that time permits, some of the steps suggested in case of longer warning periods might be applied.

STEPS THAT MIGHT BE TAKEN NOW IN PREPARATION FOR AN EARTHQUAKE WARNING

1. Communities that are vulnerable to earthquakes should develop earthquake-risk maps and maintain a record of land use in relation to risk, identifying areas and facilities that might merit critical attention in case of an earthquake warning. A community plan that identifies the earthquake-related land-use problems that probably merit priority attention in given localities should be developed.

2. Public officials in states where earthquake vulnerability is extensive may decide to initiate a state-level examination of possibilities and problems in removal, replacement, or strengthening of lifeline elements posing critical hazards in the event of an earthquake in vulnerable areas. The product could be a set of plans for collaboration among state and local jurisdictions and the private sector in the event of an earthquake prediction for various locations throughout the state. This effort would

require maximum involvement of public utility representatives and interested private groups.

3. An appropriate agency in the U.S. Department of Housing and Urban Development might be directed to study the feasibility and usefulness of a nationwide survey to ascertain patterns of land-use planning and management currently in effect in all high- and moderate-earthquake-risk areas. The survey, if undertaken, should particularly examine the extent to which earthquake hazards have been taken into account and preparation has been made to adapt land-use plans and procedures in the event of earthquake prediction.

STRUCTURAL DESIGN AND MAINTENANCE

Structural design and maintenance are the essential complement to land-use planning and management. They deal directly with the most immediate and pervasive hazards involved in earthquakes, namely, the vulnerability of man-made structures. The aim of structural design and maintenance is to ensure that all buildings occupied by human beings and all structures such as bridges and towers that might collapse on passers-by are built to conform with acceptable standards of earthquake resistance. They are also aimed at ensuring that services essential to orderly community life, such as roadways and telephone systems, will be subject to an acceptable minimum of disruption in the event of a quake. Structural design and maintenance are implemented through engineering construction, building permits, materials standards, construction guidelines, building codes and ordinances, and inspection procedures.

It is far more costly and both legally and politically more difficult to ensure that existing structures are made acceptably safe than to make new structures reasonably earthquake resistant. In the absence of a specific earthquake prediction, communities that have incorporated minimum levels of earthquake resistance into the codes governing new construction have generally been much less willing to enforce modification of old buildings. Nevertheless, insofar as legal and economic constraints are not insuperable obstacles, modification and even demolition of unsafe structures must be included in the goals of structural design and maintenance to be pursued by responsible public and private officials. Municipal, county, and state officials could lead the way by requiring their own buildings to meet acceptable standards.

Absolute invulnerability to any conceivable earthquake is unattainable, so we must speak of "earthquake-resistant" construction, and of "acceptable levels of risk." Structural engineers and legislators have been forced to rely on intuitive notions of "acceptable risk." Economists often suggest a program of cost/benefit studies as a way to identify acceptable risk levels. What are acceptable levels of risk from earthquakes? That question may turn out to be rhetorical rather than precisely answerable, but nevertheless remains crucial for structural design and maintenance programs.

The costs of making all buildings in vulnerable areas earthquake-proof will often be too great to consider. A high level of earthquake resistance for *all* structures could be a socially desirable and feasible goal in regions where potentially destructive earthquakes recur at frequent intervals. The same standard would be more difficult to justify in regions where past experience suggests that potentially destructive quakes recur only at intervals of more than a century. Accordingly, structural design and maintenance should be applied selectively to structures that are critical because of high density or occupancy rates (e.g., high-rise buildings), the nature of the populations involved (e.g., in prisons, mental hospitals, schools), or the functions served for the community (e.g., underground utilities) and that are in locations identified through microrisk mapping as especially dangerous.

Structural design and maintenance, like land-use planning and management, are chiefly continuous and long-term activities. The special value of an earthquake prediction is to permit accelerated hazard-reduction activity prior to the predicted time of occurrence and concentration of efforts in the specific locations where the danger is imminent.

Structural design and maintenance are principally responsibilities of state and local governments, requiring significant cooperation from the private sector for effective implementation. The federal government can exercise considerable indirect influence through loan and grant programs, through urban redevelopment and associated activities, and through requiring its own buildings and facilities to meet acceptable standards.

Like land-use management, structural design and maintenance are primarily applicable when there is considerable advance warning. As the period of advance warning becomes shorter, structural maintenance and the vacating of unsafe structures should be evaluated as alternative measures for saving human lives. Structural design and maintenance programs are subject to many political, legal, and economic constraints. In application, they are notorious for serving the powerful more consistently than the weak, through lax enforcement of building codes in neighborhoods inhabited by the poor. Nevertheless, because most casualties from earthquakes are likely to result from the collapse or failure of man-made structures, structural design and maintenance programs are crucial in any plan for responding constructively to earthquake predictions.

STEPS THAT MIGHT BE TAKEN WITH ONE OR SEVERAL YEARS OF ADVANCE WARNING

1. Current building codes should be reassessed at once to determine whether standards of earthquake resistance are sufficiently stringent in relation to the anticipated magnitude of the predicted quake. New construction should conform to whatever new standards are judged appropriate or should be delayed until after the quake.

2. Insofar as it is economically feasible to do so, information should be promptly assembled, indicating which structures would be relatively safe in the event of the predicted quake, which structures do not meet acceptable levels of risk, and which structures might feasibly be strengthened or otherwise modified (e.g., by removal of parapets) prior to the predicted time of the earthquake. Unless there are legal impediments, this information should be made public. Priority should be given to identifying and assessing the safety of *critical* structures.

3. All structures and systems whose functioning during and after an earthquake is essential to disaster emergency operations (e.g., emergency-operation centers, fire and police dispatch buildings, water and power control centers, telephone exchanges) that fail to meet acceptable standards of earthquake resistance should either be strengthened or relocated.

4. Community officials, with the close collaboration of private sector representatives, should initiate careful study of the practicability of bringing the various critical structures up to an acceptable standard and demolishing or changing the use of those that cannot be saved. The study should also include identification of resources that might be available to make these activities economically feasible. The resulting plan would require full cooperation and support from state and federal government agencies.

5. An appropriate public agency should be designated to advise private owners of noncritical structures concerning the vulnerability of these structures to earthquakes, procedures for bringing such structures up to acceptable standards, and the financial resources in both public and private sectors that might be available to assist the owner in upgrading the structures. The public agency designated to handle this function should work closely with appropriate business and labor leaders from the private sector.

6. When there are several years of advance warning, building departments should recommend and local governing bodies should adopt regulations and procedures to ensure that structures which meet acceptable standards of earthquake resistance are not allowed to deteriorate to the point where they no longer meet these standards.

7. Consideration should be given to requiring current seismic-risk analyses for certain categories of property within the threatened area as a condition of transfer of ownership.

8. Consideration should be given to safety standards applicable in the reconstruction period in the aftermath of a destructive earthquake, when repair, reconstruction, and demolition of many buildings and lifeline systems will be undertaken.

STEPS THAT MIGHT BE TAKEN WITH LESS THAN ONE YEAR OF ADVANCE WARNING

1. If critically hazardous structures have been identified and priorities established in advance of any earthquake prediction, and if legal obstacles have been anticipated and cleared in advance, action to strengthen, change use patterns of, or demolish a few of the most critical structures might be feasible.

2. Movable hazardous contents of buildings and facilities (e.g., toxic substances in factories) should be removed from vulnerable structures to designated safe locations outside the threatened area.

3. Consideration should be given to the removal of nonhazardous but valuable contents to safer locations. Included would be valuable records and money in financial institutions, irreplaceable documents of national and regional significance, jewelry and artwork in stores and public places, and special equipment and machinery in offices and factories. Critical records such as land titles and bank records might be reproduced on microfilm or other media.

4. Some vulnerable structures should be temporarily reinforced by such means as sandbagging walls and taping windows.

STEPS THAT MIGHT BE TAKEN NOW IN PREPARATION FOR AN EARTHQUAKE WARNING

1. Local building departments, in collaboration with appropriate state agencies and with technical advice and assistance from federal agencies, should develop plans for responding promptly in case of an earthquake prediction and should assemble and maintain current information concerning the earthquake vulnerability of critical structures in the community.

2. All federal and state agencies responsible for structures that are not under the jurisdiction of local building and safety departments should be required to develop contingency plans for responding to any earthquake warning in cooperation with local authorities.

LAUNCHING A COMPREHENSIVE PROGRAM OF PUBLIC INFORMATION AND EDUCATION

The importance of a well-conceived program of public information has already been stressed in connection with the release of predictions and the issuance of warnings (Chapter 4). Most of the residents and even the responsible public and private leaders in many areas where the risk of a destructive earthquake is substantial are quite unaware of the risk and are disposed to greet any earthquake prediction with disbelief and inaction. Even where quakes are commonplace, most of the experience is with minor earth tremors. In both types of regions earthquake prediction is an entirely new phenomenon.

Several important objectives should guide programs of public information. First, the credibility of the scientific prediction must be widely accepted before the community can respond effectively. Establishing credibility depends on clarifying the difference between scientific prediction and less valid kinds of forecasting and on conveying a realistic understanding of what is meant by probability and the chance of error. Second, the nature of earthquakes and earthquake hazard must be grasped in realistic terms so that people can appreciate the need for inconvenient and sometimes costly hazard-reduction measures. A Pollyanna view of the earthquake threat suggests that little preparation is required. A magical or sensationalist view suggests that preparation is useless. Both extremes are counterproductive so far as participation in a constructive program of earthquake preparation is concerned.

Third, people need to be kept informed about the status of the prediction. Prompt public announcement of any change in the prediction and frequent reminders when the status of the prediction is unchanged are desirable. Otherwise, the situation will breed a flurry of conflicting rumors, some contending that the prospects are much worse than people are being allowed to hear and others contending that scientists no longer believe their own prediction. Both types of rumors, if widely believed, are unsettling and may diminish reliable support for constructive programs.

Fourth, people must have a vital awareness of the steps that are being taken and of how they can cooperate in the process. Such awareness should help keep interest from lagging between issuance of the prediction and occurrence of the quake, should facilitate intelligent involvement of the populace in democratic decision making, and should promote public trust in the efforts of community leaders to prepare for the earthquake. A realistic view of the earthquake hazard, coupled with the conviction that the community's leaders are working constructively to deal with the most substantial hazards, may influence business and financial leaders to maintain their stake in the community's economic future.

In the past, educational and information campaigns about important problems have never proven spectacularly successful in America.[1] There is little reason to suppose that a major effort to inform large segments of the population about earthquakes and their prediction will fare much better, especially if traditional approaches are used. Furthermore, responsible educational efforts must compete with what may be substantially misleading depictions of disasters, human responses to disaster, and disaster planning that are often presented by the mass media of communication. Such depictions as the recent series of "disaster" motion pictures are likely to have more impact on large segments of the populace than any public educational campaign.

Nevertheless, guidelines are available for devising information programs that can play a useful part in the total earthquake-hazard-reduction effort. We offer just a few guidelines of the many available in standard sources dealing with strategies in education and information dissemination.

First, educational efforts are likely to be more effective when they relate to situations of immediate and tangible concern. Hence, we should not expect mass education and information programs launched prior to the issuance of a prediction or the occurrence of a serious earthquake to have much effect. On the other hand, a well-conceived program, launched while the initial interest aroused by prediction of a potentially destructive earthquake is high, could have considerable impact on inhabitants of the threatened area.

Second, the span of public attention and interest is normally brief unless significant new events keep the interest alive or unless people are engaged in ongoing activity connected with the topic of concern. Accordingly, one key to an effective campaign is to get as many people as possible participating early in the hazard-reduction effort.

Third, while sensational methods often seem to arouse spectacular interest, the interest is likely to be of brief duration. The effect is often to provoke irrational thinking rather than constructive responses to the threat of disaster, and the benefits derived from a less spectacular program of information are often greater.

Fourth, the most effective dissemination of information and understanding takes place through "opinion leaders" in all walks of life rather than directly to the public.[2] A campaign focused on influential leaders of

---

[1]Charles R. Wright, *Mass Communication* (New York: Random House, 1975), 2nd ed.
[2]Everett M. Rogers summarizes research on the "two-steps" flow of communication in Ithiel de Sola Pool, Wilbur Schram, Frederick W. Frye, Nathan Maccoby, and Edwin B. Parker (ed.), *Handbook of Communication* (Chicago: Rand McNally, 1973), pp. 293–295.

community groups will usually produce more cooperation with constructive programs of earthquake preparedness than indiscriminate mass communication.

STEPS THAT MIGHT BE TAKEN WITH ONE OR SEVERAL YEARS OF ADVANCE WARNING

(In addition to suggestions given here, see also the proposals in Chapter 4.)

1. Community and state leaders should invite key media representatives to collaborate with them in establishing a program for the frequent release of information on the nature of earthquakes and prediction, the current status of the prediction, preparedness programs being launched in both public and private sectors, and constructive steps for individuals and groups in the community to take.

2. A program of two-way communication should be devised with leaders from a wide array of community groups. Leaders should be helped to plan educational programs in their groups and encouraged to relay questions, concerns, and suggestions from their groups to appropriate public and private officials.

3. Special efforts should be made to reach underprivileged groups, including the more isolated ethnic, religious, non-English-speaking, aged, and nonmainstream groups in the community, regarding preparedness measures in which they might participate. Many of these groups could be reached through churches, voluntary associations, and welfare agencies.

4. Procedures (including the two-way communication already mentioned) should be developed in the threatened communities to ascertain and monitor the level of understanding about earthquake problems in the potentially affected population, and to obtain a regular and continuous feedback about steps that private individuals and groups are taking in anticipation of the quake.

5. In all communication to the affected communities, special attention should be given to the nature and importance of long-term hazard-reduction measures, such as land-use planning and management and structural design and maintenance.

6. Media that give nationwide coverage to the prediction should be encouraged to emphasize the existence of earthquake vulnerability in much of the United States and the importance of developing earthquake-preparedness programs in all vulnerable communities.

STEPS THAT MIGHT BE TAKEN WITH LESS THAN ONE YEAR OF ADVANCE WARNING

1. All of the steps suggested for longer warning periods are applicable, except for step 5. As the projected time of occurrence nears, the emphasis will shift from long-term hazard-reduction measures to emergency responses. Public announcements will be scheduled more often, and prompt and regular communication between responsible officials and mass media representatives should be assured.

2. As the predicted time approaches, warnings and instructions for public safety and welfare should be issued. Announcements would include suggestions for avoiding personal danger, for protecting fragile and valuable objects, and preparing for the immediate aftermath of the earthquake.

3. As the predicted time for the earthquake draws near, affected communities will benefit by designating some existing information centers as earthquake-information and rumor-control centers, staffed around the clock.

4. Special attention should be given to the problems of providing information on emergency developments to transients, tourists, new residents, night-shift personnel, and other groups who may not be reached by the established lines of communication.

STEPS THAT MIGHT BE TAKEN NOW IN PREPARATION FOR AN EARTHQUAKE WARNING

1. Special briefings should be held for key federal and state agency representatives and disaster planners and workers, whether public or private, to alert them to the implications of earthquake prediction and structural vulnerability. These briefings might be held in conjunction with regular disaster-related meetings of such groups as the Council of State Governments, the National Association of Civil Defense Directors, and the American National Red Cross.

2. Papers and other presentations on the implications of earthquake prediction and structural vulnerability problems should be delivered at regular professional and occupational group meetings of personnel in medicine, hospitals, the mass media, public welfare, public works, and so on.

3. Material on earthquake prediction and structural vulnerability problems should be prepared for instructional use by educational and institutional training groups such as the Defense Civil Preparedness

Agency Staff College, police and fire academies in earthquake-prone areas, school systems in earthquake-prone areas, and other interested groups.

4. Documentary films, photographic essays, and other material on earthquakes stressing effective preparedness and protective measures should be prepared for occasional use by the mass media, especially when a prediction is disseminated.

5. Officials in states where there is a significant prospect of earthquakes should invite the collaboration of local officials and representatives of the mass media in devising standby plans for communication in the event of an earthquake warning.

EVACUATING DANGEROUS LOCALITIES AND VACATING VULNERABLE STRUCTURES

Evacuation is a measure to be instituted principally as the time of the predicted event approaches, and often as a last resort when other hazard-reduction measures have not been effectively applied. Often there should be a considered choice between such measures as reinforcing a building and vacating the building and adjoining area. In some instances evacuating a limited area or vacating selected structures will be a less costly and irreversible enterprise than some of the possible land-use management and structural maintenance techniques. This may be the case particularly when there is low confidence in the prediction or when its lack of precision allows for a wide margin of error. But experience with evacuation on any but a very limited scale and for more than a very few hours or days suggests that the full social and financial costs of evacuation are often higher than originally anticipated. Hence it is very important that evacuation, when practiced, be a considered alternative to other hazard-reduction measures and not a measure adopted by default.

Weighing the advantages and disadvantages of evacuation requires an assessment of (a) the effects of evacuation on the community from which the evacuation takes place, (b) its effects on the host community, (c) its effects on the evacuees, and (d) the direct costs of the operation:

a. Depending upon who is evacuated, selective evacuation may cripple the affected community in significant ways.

b. Locating suitable host communities is often the most difficult aspect of evacuation. Evacuation for a day or two may be accomplished by dispersal, most people making their own arrangements. But for more than this brief period, and for the evacuation of large numbers, concerted relocation plans are essential, and considerable disruption to the host community can be anticipated.[3]

c. The typical candidates for evacuation—the elderly, children, and the disabled—are often those most emotionally dependent upon familiar surroundings for their sense of personal security. Evacuation often means separating family members and temporarily breaking up the groups to which people turn for support and solace in periods of stress. These emotional problems must be added to the obvious problems of economic survival produced by the separation of people from their regular place of employment.

d. The many direct costs of evacuation include transportation, temporary housing and community facilities, maintenance of order, provision of indispensable emergency facilities such as health care, protection of property left behind, and many other items.

It is probably a safe judgment that massive evacuation will rarely be an acceptable strategy for dealing with the earthquake threat. Perhaps there is an exception to this judgment in such communities as Charleston, South Carolina, and Boston, Massachusetts, where most structures are not earthquake-resistant and, in the event of a strong quake, are therefore a threat both to their occupants and to passers-by. But even here, massive evacuation could probably be given serious consideration only if the time window for prediction could be narrowed to a few days. But *selective evacuation* and systematic *vacating* of unsafe structures will certainly be an essential part of any complete response to earthquake prediction. Evacuation is clearly the most appropriate response where no other hazard-reduction measures are feasible, as with the threat of tsunamis and landslides. After all feasible preparatory efforts have been made, some unsafe structures are bound to remain, and some inappropriate land use is sure to defy all efforts at correction. Vacating these buildings and evacuating the specifically identified areas of greatest risk will be a crucial task in saving lives.

---

[3]See C. J. Lammers, *Studies in Holland Flood Disaster, 1953: Survey of Evacuation Problems and Disaster Experiences,* Vol. II (Washington, D.C.: Committee on Disaster Studies, National Research Council–National Academy of Sciences, 1956); Samuel Z. Klausner and Harry V. Kincaid, *Social Problems of Sheltering Flood Evacuees* (New York: Bureau of Applied Social Research, Columbia University, 1956); Fred C. Iklé and Harry V. Kincaid, *Social Aspects of Wartime Evacuation of American Cities* (Washington, D.C.: Committee on Disaster Studies, National Academy of Sciences–National Research Council, Publication 393, 1956); and Eleanor H. Bernert and Fred C. Iklé, "Evacuation and the Cohesion of Urban Groups," *American Journal of Sociology,* 58 (1952), 133–138.

STEPS THAT MIGHT BE TAKEN WITH ONE OR SEVERAL YEARS OF ADVANCE WARNING

1. A careful study should be initiated to determine what areas, facilities, and buildings at risk might best be handled by evacuation. The study should identify waterfront areas within potential reach of tsunamis,[4] land areas vulnerable to landslides, localities that are especially vulnerable because of geological structure or proximity to the predicted point of impact for the earthquake, facilities that endanger the occupants because they may not perform well under the stress of an earthquake, and unsafe structures that are unlikely to be reinforced or demolished. Priority attention should be given to critical structures, as defined earlier in the chapter.

2. Prototype plans for selective evacuation and for "staying put" should be prepared and studied, so as to develop the optimal combination in the stand-by plan. The determination of an optimal plan should be made by public officials after extensive input has been received from citizens and organizations in the private sector.

3. Whatever plans are adopted should be integrated so far as possible with existing and developing disaster plans.

STEPS THAT MIGHT BE TAKEN WITH LESS THAN ONE YEAR OF ADVANCE WARNING

1. Whatever is feasible from the preceding steps should be attempted in case of briefer warning times.

2. Insofar as it is feasible in light of the duration of the time window for the predicted occurrence of the quake, the following should be evacuated or vacated: waterfront areas potentially vulnerable to tsunamis, land areas subject to landslide danger, localities that are especially vulnerable because of geologic structure or proximity to the predicted point of impact, areas especially susceptible to unmanageable fire, areas downstream from potentially unsafe dams in which the water level has not been sufficiently lowered, hospitals and other institutions that have been identified as possibly vulnerable, facilities that may not perform well with consequent danger to structures and surrounding areas, and previously identified hazardous structures.

---

[4]This was done in Hilo, Hawaii, as reported in William A. Anderson, "Tsunami Warning in Crescent City, California, and Hilo, Hawaii," *The Great Alaska Earthquake of 1964: Human Ecology,* Committee on the Alaska Earthquake, National Research Council (Washington, D.C.: National Academy of Sciences, 1970), pp. 116–124.

STEPS THAT MIGHT BE TAKEN NOW IN PREPARATION FOR AN EARTHQUAKE WARNING

1. As part of the general emergency plan for each community and state, there should be feasibility studies of alternative plans for selective evacuation involving temporary relocation within the community and outside the community. The plan should indicate what locations, resources, and facilities, if any, might be available and suitable for temporary relocation of evacuees for both brief and extended periods of time.

REDUCING SPECIAL HAZARDS TO THE COMMUNITY

Each community will differ from every other in the unique set of potentially hazardous facilities and conditions with which the residents must cope. Many of these unique hazards have to do with community lifelines. For example, some communities are dependent upon aqueducts to convey the water supply from distant locations, often crossing and recrossing fault lines. Communities that depend on a very few highways, roads, or railway lines for daily supplies of food and other necessities will be especially concerned about the vulnerability of these transportation lines. Bridges and subway systems are crucial transportation links. The extent to which a community depends on locally stored or piped-in oil, coal, natural gas, electricity, or other fuels will indicate where the main dangers may lie in maintaining needed energy supplies in the anticipated emergency.

There are other special hazards not connected with lifelines. Fire has often been the principal secondary source of property damage and loss of life. Besides attempting to control the source of fires (such as ruptured gas lines and high-voltage electric power lines), responsible officials will be concerned about conditions that facilitate the unchecked spread of fire, such as highly flammable brushlands adjacent to the community and concentrations of wooden structures. A dam upstream from populated areas can pose a special threat. While nuclear plants are generally built to exacting safety standards, they will sometimes merit special attention from the community. Manufacture, storage, and transportation facilities involving explosive, highly flammable, toxic, or chemically reactive materials can be a threat to the community.

Many of these potential hazards will be under private control in the realm of public utilities, or under state or federal control. In many of these instances the city or county will not have the direct authority to deal with the hazard that they have over private business and residential structures. Hence it is essential that local officials seek the voluntary cooperation of agencies in control of such facilities, and that all federal and state agencies and public utilities be responsible for assessing and working to minimize whatever potential hazards their facilities may pose for local communities.

STEPS THAT MIGHT BE TAKEN WITH LONG OR SHORT PERIODS OF ADVANCE WARNING

1. As the predicted time of occurrence for the earthquake approaches, local officials, responsible officials in state and federal agencies, public utility officials, and responsible business and industrial leaders should make judgments of the feasibility and desirability of executing as many of the following actions as may be appropriate, taking into account the duration of the time window for the prediction:

Shut off natural gas pipelines
Shut off petroleum pipelines
Divert traffic from bridges with approaches that might be damaged and unusable
Shut down vulnerable sections of subway systems
Reschedule departures from work to avoid rush-hour bottleneck traffic
Draw down reservoirs behind vulnerable dams
Create firebreaks to impede the spread of fire through highly flammable brushlands or concentrations of highly flammable structures
Take other protective measures against fire hazard
Take protective measures against pollution hazards such as the rupture of sewage lines
Close off incompressible fluid lines
Reduce or remove supplies of fuels and hazardous chemicals in storage tanks
Suspend operations in all factories and other facilities where operations would be hazardous in case of a destructive quake
Shut down nuclear reactors and hydroelectric power plants when circumstances warrant
Clear harbors of ships that may be endangered in the event of a tsunami

STEPS THAT MIGHT BE TAKEN NOW IN PREPARATION FOR AN EARTHQUAKE WARNING

1. As part of general emergency planning, each community should maintain a current inventory of all special potentially hazardous facilities

and should make plans for dealing with them in case of long- and short-term earthquake warnings.

2. All federal and state agencies and public utilities operating in earthquake-vulnerable areas should make a continuing assessment of the risk to communities in the event of damage in a severe earthquake, and develop plans for reducing the hazard in case of long- and short-term earthquake predictions.

READYING EMERGENCY SERVICES

Communities subject to the risk of earthquake already have—or should have—emergency plans for working expeditiously and effectively in the aftermath of a destructive earthquake. An earthquake prediction provides a heretofore unavailable opportunity to ensure that emergency forces and resources are in a state of maximum readiness when the quake occurs. By indicating in advance the magnitude and location of the quake, the prediction can be very helpful to emergency personnel. Long prediction time windows remain a problem, however. The extent to which emergency forces can be placed and maintained on alert status will depend on the duration of the prediction time window. The maximum benefit will accrue when seismologists are able to specify the time of occurrence within a period of a few days, or when the long-term prediction can be supplemented by detection of immediately precursory signs a few hours before the quake. Whether the latter can soon be achieved in case of severe earthquakes is not yet known.

Because the states of California and Alaska have had abundant experience in handling emergency services in major quakes, and reports of their experience are available to other states, there is no need to go into detail here concerning the nature of emergency planning. We note in passing that major problem areas include search and rescue, servicing medical needs, insuring backup for essential facilities and life-sustaining systems, and achieving interorganizational coordination.

STEPS THAT MIGHT BE TAKEN WITH ONE OR SEVERAL YEARS OF ADVANCE WARNING

1. Public and private emergency services in the community should develop schedules so that each of the steps in readying services for post-disaster work will take place at an optimal time. For example, it would be wasteful to begin stockpiling emergency supplies long before they are needed, and it would be counterproductive to place emergency forces on alert status before the period of danger.

2. Plans should be developed to involve individuals from the threatened communities in both preparatory and postdisaster activities, by setting up training classes in first aid, in search and rescue operations, and in survival techniques, and through various other steps. These plans, too, should be carefully scheduled, usually so that maximum activity occurs shortly before the projected quake. For example, the lessons of first aid will be applied most effectively when the emergency occurs soon after these lessons have been learned.

STEPS THAT MIGHT BE TAKEN WITH LESS THAN ONE YEAR OF ADVANCE WARNING

1. Emergency plans for search and rescue and rehabilitation should be reviewed and adapted in light of the predicted place, time, and magnitude of the quake and in light of the existing critical and hazardous facilities in the community.

2. Full preparation should be made for the quake, including stockpiling essential equipment and supplies in safe but accessible locations, briefing and organizing emergency personnel, testing the adequacy of communication and coordination among the various public and private agencies involved in emergency operations, and planning for the constructive use of individual volunteers.

STEPS THAT MIGHT BE TAKEN NOW IN PREPARATION FOR AN EARTHQUAKE WARNING

1. Existing emergency plans in earthquake-prone communities should be reviewed and revised to incorporate plans for responding to both short- and long-term earthquake predictions.

DEALING WITH COUNTERPRODUCTIVE CONSEQUENCES OF PREDICTION

On a purely speculative basis, it is possible to conceive of various counterproductive consequences that could develop following the prediction of an earthquake. These might include economic disruption and decline in the threatened communities; heightened conflict among various interest groups in the area[5]; loss of trust in political officials and political forms; widespread anxiety resulting from the anticipation of the earth-

[5]R. R. Dynes and E. L. Quarantelli, *Community Conflict: Its Absence and Presence in Natural Disasters,* Preliminary Paper 18, Disaster Research Center (Columbus, Ohio: The Ohio State University, 1975).

quake disaster (which, in extreme cases, may aggravate mental illness); and panic flight from the threatened area. There is no assurance that any of these conditions will actually occur to a significant degree. Indeed, past experience leads us to believe that such effects are grossly exaggerated and stereotyped in much of the current thinking about the economic, political, social, and psychological consequences of earthquake predictions. The completion of several major investigations now under way will supply more information than we now have, especially about economic consequences of earthquake predictions.[6]

The potentially counterproductive economic and political consequences of earthquake prediction have already been discussed in two previous chapters (Chapters 5 and 8), so further discussion is unnecessary here, except to remind public officials of three important considerations. First, some forms of federal assistance to communities that have to deal with the consequences of earthquake predictions may already be available under PL 93-288, the Disaster Relief Act of 1974.[7] Second, a long period of advance warning affords many opportunities to handle adjustments in the local economy in an orderly way. And third, the development of constructive economic and political response depends upon involving key business, labor, and other community leaders in planning from the moment a serious prediction is released.

In visualizing possible counterproductive social and psychological consequences of earthquake predictions and warnings, public officials may fear panic flight from the threatened area. They may be haunted by

---

[6]The National Science Foundation is currently funding three technology assessments of earthquake prediction: (1) Institute of Behavioral Science, University of Colorado, "Socioeconomic and Political Consequences of Earthquake Prediction," J. Eugene Haas and Dennis S. Mileti, Co-Principal Investigators, February 18, 1975, from February 1, 1975, to February 29, 1976, Contract No. AEN 7424079; (2) Stanford Research Institute, "A Technology Assessment of Earthquake Prediction," Leo W. Weisbecker and Thomas J. Logothetti, Co-Principal Investigators, March 21, 1974, from June 1, 1974, to November 30, 1975, Contract No. ERP 7406934; and (3) New England Bureau, Inc., "A Mini Technology Assessment Study of Earthquake Prediction Techniques and their Applications," Martin V. Jones, Principal Investigator, June 11, 1974, from June 1, 1974, to May 31, 1975, Contract No. GI 43739.

[7]Under the provisions of PL 93-288, the President has the authority to provide technical assistance to states in developing comprehensive plans and practicable programs for preparation against disaster, including hazard reduction, avoidance, and mitigation. Under the "emergency assistance" provisions of that law, the President may also provide predisaster assistance to save lives and protect property and public health and safety. The President's authority to provide predisaster aid for such broad programs as building demolition, repair and reconstruction, and land-use planning and management is probably not sufficient under the provisions of current law; thus PL 93-288 may require amendment or supplementary legislation.

the specter of thousands of people rushing to get away from the city, with the result that all highways, railroads, and other transportation facilities are immobilized. Social scientists who have studied disasters use the term "panic" in a very specific sense to refer to an acute fear reaction marked by loss of self-control and followed by nonsocial and nonrational flight.[8] Defined in this way, research has shown that panic is a rare response even under conditions of actual disaster threat and impact. Only a few scattered cases of individual and small-group panic have been found in the several hundred disasters studied in the past 25 years.[9] In the few cases where it has occurred, there is an intense fear of immediate danger accompanied by the perception that the escape routes from the danger area are closing. It is evident that panic should not be a problem when a long-term warning is issued.

The possibility of more rational, controlled forms of flight behavior, including informal evacuation of the threatened area as the time of the predicted quake approaches, presents a much more likely problem that should be taken into account in disaster-preparedness contingency plans and preparations. Plans to handle this potential development would include the following: (a) identify and publicize the safe locations within the community or threatened area; (b) develop a careful evacuation plan, placing special emphasis on the modes of transportation to be used, mechanisms for monitoring and directing people over the most appropriate routes of egress, and adequate preparations to receive evacuees in the host communities and facilities; (c) assign organizational responsibilities to the civil defense, police, fire department, National Guard units, and so on, in providing instructions and guidance to the public on the kinds of precautionary and protective actions people should take in the event of various contingencies; (d) develop a feedback information system that keeps key decision makers informed on how the public is responding to the predictions and warnings; and (e) provide the means for prompt dissemination of relevant information concerning the prediction and warning to the threatened populace and concerning the precautionary and protective actions they need to take in order to minimize deaths, injuries, property destruction, and social disruption.

Panic in the broader sense includes such practices as "panic buying"— i.e., needlessly stockpiling certain items of merchandise until artificial shortages are created. These reactions are not uncommon in periods of crisis, but fortunately they are often of only passing significance. They

---

[8] E. L. Quarantelli, "The Nature and Conditions of Panic," *American Journal of Sociology*, 60(3) (November 1954), 267–275.

[9] E. L. Quarantelli, "Human Behavior in Disasters" in *Conference Proceedings: Design to Survive Disaster* (Chicago: IIT Research Institute, 1973), pp. 53–74.

are least likely to occur or to be of serious consequence when (a) all relevant information flows freely to the general public without delay; (b) procedures are promptly established to ensure the equitable distribution of items that are becoming scarce; and (c) leaders in the public and private sectors inspire public confidence that they are taking all reasonable steps to alleviate shortages and other inconveniences to which people are exposed.

An additional fear of public officials is that earthquake predictions and warnings may produce high levels of anxiety, emotional disturbances, and mental disorders in the affected populace. The best available evidence from previous wartime and peacetime disasters suggest that this fear is unfounded.[10] In response to the actual impact of disaster, emotional aftereffects are widespread but relatively transitory. Anxiety remains within manageable bounds for most people and results in few or no new cases of mental illness in the population.[11] Similarly, experience with other crises suggests that most people will deal with anxiety-provoking anticipation of disaster following an earthquake prediction by *normalizing* the situation (see Chapter 4) and that new cases of mental illness will be rare. Nevertheless, until we have experienced several instances of earthquake warning, practitioners and agencies in the health fields should establish procedures for monitoring the rates and kinds of mental disorders during the period after an earthquake warning to determine what, if any, special problems require their attention.

Perhaps the most common and prevalent counterproductive response to earthquake predictions and warnings will derive from the "normalcy bias" mentioned in the previous paragraph and discussed in greater detail in Chapter 4. Both responsible officials and the general public in the affected area are likely to accept uncritically any information that enables them to disbelieve the prediction, minimize the danger, and view the situation optimistically. There is likely to be sufficient ambiguity in earthquake predictions and warnings, especially the ones released during the next few years, to allow people to convince themselves either that no real danger exists or that the danger is so far in the future that they can defer taking any type of precautionary or protective action. This common tendency to deny the danger or to become complacent about it poses a major challenge to officials in utilizing earthquake predictions and warnings in such a manner as to produce the needed hazard-reduc-

[10]Irving L. Janis, *Air War and Emotional Stress: Psychological Studies of Bombing and Civil Defense* (New York: McGraw-Hill Book Co., 1951).
[11]Verta Taylor, Alex Ross, and E. L. Quarantelli, *The Delivery of Mental Health Services in Disasters,* Disaster Research Center (Columbus, Ohio: The Ohio State University, 1975).

tion and disaster-preparedness plans and programs. The responsible federal, state, and local officials must take major responsibility for planning and implementing these programs and for facilitating public compliance with their requirements. More specific suggestions for dealing with the normalcy bias have been offered in Chapter 4.

THE PROSPECTS FOR CONSTRUCTIVE RESPONSE

While predictions will inescapably bring negative as well as positive results, the contents of this chapter have demonstrated that many significantly constructive measures will become possible with the advent of earthquake prediction. With reasonable advance planning, the immediate prospect for saving lives is striking. The full potential for reducing property loss may be realized more slowly, as we learn to anticipate and deal effectively with attendant economic, legal, and political processes. But even here, much can be done with the first credible prediction.

The experience with hurricanes suggests the positive results to be anticipated. Procedures for responding to hurricane warnings have been steadily improved in the United States over a period of years. Emergency forces have learned how to evacuate thousands of people for a few crucial days. Protective measures have been devised for minimizing property loss. Overall savings in lives and property on the basis of hurricane warnings have been impressive.[12] With careful planning, the gains made possible by earthquake predictions should be equally or even more impressive.

---

[12]The hurricane-warning system in the United States is generally given credit for the decreasing loss of human life from the combined physical effects of hurricanes (winds, floods, and storm surges). The dollar value of physical damage has rapidly increased because of the accelerating residential and commercial development along the hurricane-prone Atlantic and Gulf coasts. During the last decade the rate of capital development in these vulnerable areas was more than three times that for the United States as a whole. However, the hurricane-warning system is estimated to save about $25 million during an average season. See Gilbert F. White and J. Eugene Haas, *Assessment of Research on Natural Hazards* (Cambridge, Mass.: The MIT Press, 1975), pp. 242–255. Also see Office of Emergency Preparedness, Executive Office of the President, "Hurricanes and Storm Surges," *Disaster Preparedness,* Vol. III, Chapter C (Washington, D.C.: U.S. Government Printing Office, 1972), pp. 39–51.

SELECTED REFERENCES

Anderson, William A. "Tsunami Warning in Crescent City, California and Hilo, Hawaii," *The Great Alaska Earthquake of 1964: Human Ecology,* Committee on the Alaska Earthquake, National Research Council. Washington, D.C.: National Academy of Sciences, 1970.

Bernert, Eleanor H., and Fred C. Iklé. "Evacuation and the Cohesion of Urban Groups," *American Journal of Sociology,* 58 (1952), 133–138.

Dynes, Russell R., and E. L. Quarantelli. *Community Conflict: Its Absence and Presence in Natural Disasters,* Preliminary Paper 18, Disaster Research Center. Columbus, Ohio: The Ohio State University, 1975.

Haas, J. Eugene. "Forecasting the Consequences of Earthquake Forecasting," *Social Science Perspectives on the Coming San Francisco Earthquake: Economic Impact, Prediction, and Reconstruction,* Natural Hazard Research Working Paper No. 25. Boulder, Colo.: University of Colorado, Institute of Behavioral Science, 1974.

Iklé, Fred C., and Harry V. Kincaid. *Social Aspects of Wartime Evacuation of American Cities,* Committee on Disaster Studies, National Research Council, Publication 393. Washington, D.C.: National Academy of Sciences, 1956.

Janis, Irving L. *Air War and Emotional Stress: Psychological Studies of Bombing and Civil Defense.* New York: McGraw-Hill Book Co., 1951.

Klausner, Samuel Z., and Harry V. Kincaid. *Social Problems of Sheltering Flood Evacuees,* Bureau of Applied Social Research. New York: Columbia University, 1956.

Lammers, C. J. *Studies in Holland Flood Disaster, 1953: Survey of Evacuation Problems and Disaster Experiences,* Vol. II, Committee on Disaster Studies, National Research Council. Washington, D.C.: National Academy of Sciences, 1956.

Pool, Ithiel de Sola, Wilbur Schram, Frederick W. Frye, Nathan Maccoby, and Edwin B. Parker (ed.). *Handbook of Communication.* Chicago: Rand McNally, 1973. pp. 293–295.

Quarantelli, E. L. "Human Behavior in Disasters," *Conference Proceedings: Design to Survive Disaster.* Chicago: IIT Research Institute, 1973. 53–74.

Quarantelli, E. L. "The Nature and Conditions of Panic," *American Journal of Sociology,* 60(3) (November 1954), 267–275.

Taylor, Verta, Alex Ross, and E. L. Quarantelli. *The Delivery of Mental Health Services in Disasters,* Disaster Research Center. Columbus, Ohio: The Ohio State University, 1975.

White, Gilbert F., and J. Eugene Haas. *Assessment of Research on Natural Hazards.* Cambridge, Mass.: The MIT Press, 1975.

Wright, Charles R. *Mass Communication,* 2nd ed. New York: Random House, 1975.